BOATING FOR SPORTSMEN

BOATING FOR SPORTSMEN

by Jim Emmett and Jack Seville

Outdoor Life • Harper & Row
New York

Manufactured in the United States of America

CONTENTS

INTRODUCTION

THE OUTDOORSMAN's most important piece of equipment, and his largest investment, is his boat and boating equipment. It represents, by far, the greatest expenditure for outdoor recreation, and the total investment nationally is multiplying faster than all of the other categories of sporting equipment.

Sportsmen are a mobile group, always on the go—to better fishing, sportier hunting, more remote campsites. And their equipment, ideally, has to be just as mobile. Their boats have to be light enough to carry on top of the car, small enough to fit in the back of a station wagon, or maneuverable enough to travel on a trailer.

We have attempted to keep this from being just another boating book. As a distillation of a combined sixty years of experience, the authors hope to offer a primer on what is available, the selection, care, use, and most of all, the enjoyment of boats for sport. If the following pages prove to be a little help to a lot of our fellow outdoorsmen, or a lot of help to a few, we will be richly rewarded.

Jim Emmett, Annapolis, Md.
Jack Seville, Malvern, Pa.

1 Design and Construction

To GIVE truly satisfactory service, a boat must be suited to the task it is called upon to perform. A craft that will please the New England offshore fisherman won't suit the man whose angling is confined to a comparatively sheltered inland lake. Neither will a big deep-V hull that permits an angler to fish the Gulf Stream be ideal on the bonefish flats of the Florida Keys.

To appreciate the complexity of hull design and to be better qualified to choose the type of boat which will serve you best, you should learn to identify the various hull forms and know something about their effect on performance.

A *displacement hull* plows through the water. With much of its surface in continuous contact with the water, the boat's speed is restricted by friction. When the hull reaches its maximum speed, additional power will only increase the turbulence in the flow of water over its surface. Within its low-speed range, it has inherent seaworthiness, but over-powering can be dangerous.

A *planing hull* rises on top of the water as power is applied; the wetted area is reduced and skin friction is denied the opportunity to build up. But in attaining its maximum speed, the planing hull must make a sacrifice to seaworthiness.

There are three basic shapes which designers work with—flat bottom, V bottom, and round bottom. Each of these shapes has its own particular characteristics both at rest and when propelled. By using combinations of these shapes a designer hopes to achieve particular results—a hull for a specific purpose.

While cost is a big factor in setting hull shapes, particularly in the lower-priced boats, skillful designing and manufacturing can produce a boat of practically any configuration. The advances that benefit boatmen come from a sound blending of shapes and their characteristics with materials and their properties.

Even experienced boatmen can be puzzled by today's hull designs and their sometimes radical appearance.

1

As perplexing as some hulls may appear, boatmen should keep an open mind concerning the efforts of designers to provide better-performing craft. True, the common complaint that "it just doesn't look like a boat" is sometimes justified. Yet, out of such modern designs, developments are emerging which will eventually benefit all boat owners.

FLAT BOTTOMS

Those who want flashy performance and sleek appearance, often deride flat-bottomed craft, claiming them to be slow, unseaworthy, bad pounders, and ungainly. The fact is that more fish have likely been caught from such boats than from any other type. It's true that a flat-bottomed hull pounds more than other types, but those other alleged drawbacks are not necessarily legitimate.

Flat-bottomed craft, whether constructed of wood, plywood, or aluminum, are the easiest to build, taking less time, less know-how, and simpler facilities. Accordingly, they cost less than other hulls of matching size. This becomes more apparent, and more important, as one works up to bigger boats. Included in this category are craft, notably dory modifications and garveys, that are highly seaworthy. Appearance is a matter of good designing and of keeping within the limitations set by the hull's shape and size.

Aside from the scow with its angular bottom lines, the simplest hull form here is the punt, which is similar to prams and the larger johnboats. These boats are exceptionally stable and excellent load carriers. Ordinarily, they're slow, meant to be driven economically up to around six miles an hour, and best suited for sheltered waters. But there are exceptions.

The skiff design undoubtedly resulted as an improvement of the snub-nosed pram. The sharp bow means that much less bottom to pound and possibly improves the boat's appearance. But a sharp bow in this case also means some loss in stability and load-carrying qualities. These faults hardly show up in the ordinary 12 to 14-foot sizes, but smaller skiffs can be cranky. In any size, the shape of the stern determines the skiff's rowing qualities and its performance with a motor. For use with oars, the stern should be narrow, the transom out of the water, and the bottom curved upward to it. A model intended to drive faster than the usual six m.p.h. speed will have a box-like stern with a wide, low transom and a more or less straight keel astern. You just can't make a slow skiff fast by hitching a big motor on its transom. The stern goes down and the bow up, but there's no appreciable increase in speed. Placing more weight forward helps some, but the hull is still a displacement type, ploughing through the water rather than riding up on it.

The dory, while flat-bottomed with a displacement-type hull, shows different design features. Dories achieved their reputation of being exceptionally seaworthy in the big sizes, around 20 feet and with plenty of beef handling the oars. Reduce this size appreciably, still retain the narrow bottom, flaring sides, and high V transom characteristic of the true dory, and you

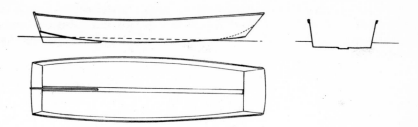

Punt has hull similar to prams, johnboats. Stable and good load carriers, the bows of these boats are sometimes rounded.

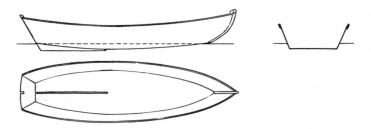

Dory rowing model has narrow transom. This hull, when modified for outboard-motor power, would have boxy stern with low, wide transom.

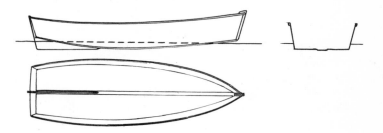

Flat-Bottomed Skiff

Cabin dory has flat bottom, draws little water. Its typical length is 22 feet.

have a relatively tender craft. Also, aside from the difficulty of mounting the motor, the boat is slow under power. However, such modifications as a lower and fuller stern avoid these faults. The inherent seaworthiness of the type is largely retained, and the design utilizes motor power very satisfactorily. Easy rowing, however, is sacrificed.

It is in the big-boat field that the greatest progress has been made in flat-bottomed craft. This is being accomplished by some of our better boat designers who feel there's a need for plain utilitarian-type craft which can be produced at low or moderate cost by either amateur or professional builders.

Cabin dories, from 16 to 22 feet, which have the shape characteristics of the pram, make fine fishing and utility craft that can be powered to give water-skiing speeds. Even in larger sizes, these flat-bottomed hulls draw very little water and are able to manipulate shallows that would stop round or V-bottomed hulls of matching size.

V BOTTOMS

The V-bottomed hull design, as originally developed, was meant to avoid the chief faults of the flat-bottomed type. Further improving, however, triggered largely by the increase in horsepower available, resulted in the flat-aft planing hull now common for fast outboards.

In its simplest form, the V-bottomed skiff or auto-top merely has a semi-V bottom. In small models, the halves of the bottom may even be curved rather than flat to afford some of the advantages of the round-bottomed hull. In any case, the resultant shape gives a slightly sharper forefoot, which lessens pounding when bucking a chop under power. Also, the greater depth contributes to seaworthiness as does the shape astern in the cases of a following sea. A disadvantage is the higher building cost, if only because of the molded bottom shape. While this simple V-bottomed skiff will drive economically up to a certain speed, it is still a displacement hull, one that pushes or ploughs through the water.

The contemporary V-bottomed boat is a planing hull, designed to skim on the surface with maximum speed, economy, and safety. While there are innumerable makes or models in this classification, such a boat can be considered as combining the good features of the ordinary V-bottom—a sharp forefoot or entrance—with the broad flat after underbody of the flat-bottomed skiff. But here the comparison ends, for the modern V-bottom design is accentuated and refined. For example, the sharpness of the forward V is extreme and the bottom sections centrally on each side have become hollow rather than flat. Additionally, the topsides are likely to show considerable flare forward, continued possibly into an overhanging bow. At high speed, the boat should plane, riding on the flat of the bottom aft with the sharp forefoot merely cutting waves. Spray should be deflected by the flared topsides and, in the form of water and air, be carried aft by the hollow of the bottom to afford some lifting effect.

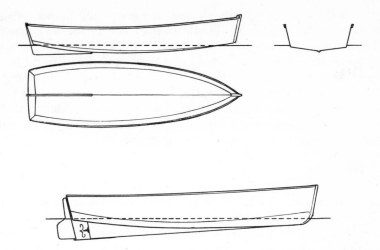

V-bottomed skiff has slightly sharper forefoot, pounds less than flat-bottomed hull.

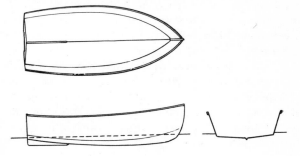

V-bottomed auto-top is similar to skiff (above) though keel is sometimes arched.

V-bottomed runabout has planing hull with sharp forefoot that flattens at stern.

More recently, the trend, notably for 18-footers and larger boats, has been in another direction—toward hulls having a deep V for the entire length of the bottom.

Here the effort is to provide a boat that can maintain its speed in rough water without excessive pounding. The chines (where bottom and sides meet) are out of the water and the deep V extends the entire length of the bottom. Beyond this the bottom configuration may be quite complex. For example, a series of longitudinal steps may be provided to lift and keep the deep hull stable at high speeds and in choppy water.

ROUND BOTTOMS

Some round-bottomed runabouts and fast auto-top boats are virtually V-bottomed hulls with the chines rounded off. This helps in giving the hull that flatness aft which, along with widening the stern, provides an effective afterbearing surface for utilizing power. In comparison, a rowing model will show much easier lines, be slacker bilged, as it's called. The hull will also be slimmer, especially astern. Understandably, an all-purpose model will be a compromise shape, somewhere between these extremes.

The slacker the curve on a round-bottom the trickier the boat may be to get into and out of. This, however, is called initial stability, and a boat should not be condemned in this respect. The same boat may have exceptionally good final stability, meaning that in actual use, especially in choppy water, it will be stable and seaworthy. This feature is more likely to show up, and be more important, in a big boat than in a small one. For example, the large round-bottomed lapstrakes are preferred by many fishermen for exposed waters because, along with riding more softly than the average V-bottomed hull, the period of rolling is slower and the boat rolls with less snap.

If you're interested in canoes, this effect of the amount of round to the hull's sections and the fore-and-aft curvature on the craft's handling qualities is worth understanding. The canoe in the accompanying sketch is for expert canoeists, an extreme model designed essentially for rapids and crooked streams. The cross section of the center shows a rounded bottom that makes for speed rather than stability. The bottom lines have considerable rise fore and aft, enabling the course of the canoe to be changed quickly. There is no tumblehome (opposite of flare) or inward round at any point, permitting flaring the sides toward the ends to throw off waves in heavy rapids. A more conventional model, shown with dotted lines, will have a flatter bottom with some tumblehome to the sides. The keel will be rockered only toward the extreme ends. Also, in comparison with the river model, the canoe will be fuller-ended. Such a canoe is more stable and a better load carrier. You won't be able to turn it as quickly, but it will be easier for you to maintain a straight course with it.

In the big outboard and stern-drive field, the modern round-bottomed boat is likely to be fast as well as seaworthy. While there is a wide variety of

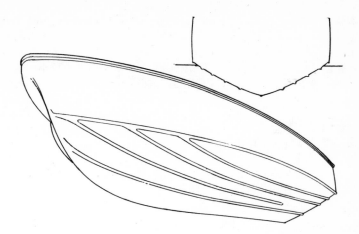

Deep V-bottom is modern design with V-shape running full length of hull.

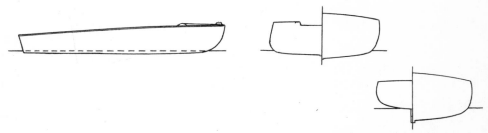

Round-bottomed auto-top is a V-bottomed hull with chines rounded off. Two drawings at right show bow and stern views. The rowing model has narrower transom than hull designed for outboard-motor power.

Round-bottomed sea skiff can be adapted to stern drive, inboard-outboard power.

Canoe built for rapids, as compared with conventional model (dotted lines).

models, a fishing boat of this sort will usually show sea skiff characteristics with modifications to provide a hull that will be able in rough water and capable of utilizing power effectively. Whether built of wood, fiberglass, or even formed aluminum, the hull is likely to be a lapstrake type. The raised edges act as a series of longitudinal steps to achieve a lifting effect.

MULTIHULLS

Many of today's hull designs defy classification. Some are multihulled, often showing some complex bottom configuration, utilizing the features of the suspension-type competition hulls. Such sculpturing of the bottom and removing the flat, hard shape can increase speed and improve the rough-water performance of hulls 16 feet and longer. One design retains the deep forefoot of the modern V-bottomed outboard, but provides twin side hulls or sponsons. Lateral stability is gained, the boat is less tippy, and pounding should be reduced along with the boat being fast and able in rough water. Another design utilizes the catamaran or twin-hulls idea, providing two riding surfaces plus a tunnel which gives a lifting effect. Or, to double this tunnel lift, the trimaran or three-hulls idea is used.

You have another set of variables to contend with in choosing the best boat for your service. Shall it be wood, fiberglass, aluminum, or a combination of these materials?

WOOD BOATS

Plywood boats are low priced. Especially in a large boat, you can get a lot of boat for your money. Being reasonably lightweight, the smaller sizes can be car carried, the larger ones readily handled with a trailer. The boats stand up well in such service and shouldn't be weakened by dry storage.

Maintenance is comparatively simple, assuming that the manufacturer used a proper finishing technique, and these boats are durable. Simple damage, such as gouges or deep scratches, are easily concealed in repainting; more serious damage can generally be made good with common hand tools.

In tightness, ease of maintenance, and durability, a plywood boat can be improved by covering the bottom, or even the complete hull, with fiberglass. This is a worthwhile extra feature offered by some builders. If the boat is fiberglassed later, the finish must be removed. Bare plywood holds fiberglass exceptionally well.

While panel-plywood boats are built from sections of ready-made, laminated panels, the molded-plywood craft is quite another story. A molded plywood hull is built of strips of thin veneer that have been treated with phenolic resin. These pieces of veneer are temporarily secured crisscross over a form that's shaped exactly like the inside of the desired hull, and three to five layers are built up.

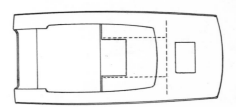

Catamaran has two riding surfaces plus a tunnel between which affords lifting effect.

Three-point hull has deep forefoot of V-bottom with two side hulls or sponsons for lateral stability.

Trimaran has two tunnels to double lift effect.

Molded-plywood boats are reasonably lightweight, and have no seams—except at the transom. The smaller models are fine for auto-top carrying, the larger ones for trailering. Whether the boat is painted or varnished may be important. Any varnished surface is more affected by weather and wear, and requires more frequent and more careful refinishing. For fishing and general use, a painted boat of this sort serves best. For purely pleasure use, it's hard to beat the looks of a varnished mahogany model.

DOUBLE PLANKED

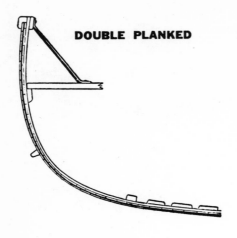

Synthetic sandwiched between two layers of planking makes light and strong hull.

LAPSTRAKE

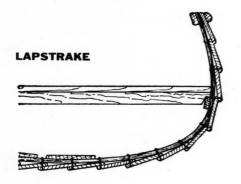

Use of plywood and new fastening methods make this type of boat a favorite.

PLYWOOD

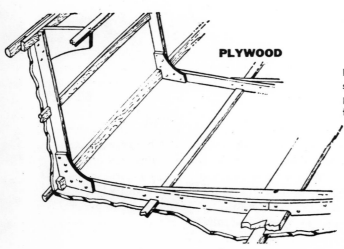

Large plywood panels and construction details like this make possible the building of large and fairly inexpensive craft.

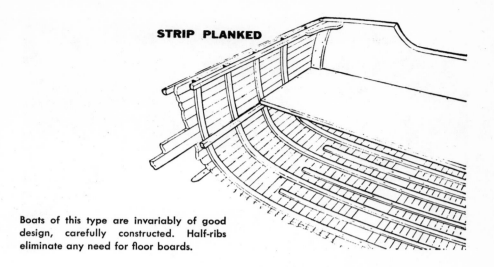

STRIP PLANKED

Boats of this type are invariably of good design, carefully constructed. Half-ribs eliminate any need for floor boards.

Although lapstrake (or clinker) construction—in which planks overlap at the edges—is one of the oldest forms of boatbuilding, these craft continue to maintain their popularity. Lapstrake boats are able craft and good performers. Invariably they're honestly built, and mostly they're kept plain in appearance and finish, as is proper for boats likely to see utilitarian service. And while hull shapes have been altered over the years to keep pace with the constant increase in power, the big difference between today's lapstrake boats and those of the past is in the planking—what's used and how it's fastened. A few top-notch builders continue to use mahogany. But traditional white cedar for planking has largely been displaced by plywood. However, panels of sound core construction must be used.

Nowadays, less reliance is put on the traditional copper rivets for fastening planks, largely to get away from their tendency to stretch. Some builders use copper rivets in combination with bronze screws, and at least one manufacturer uses tiny machine bolts that can be tightened. Today's builders also have the advantage of better compounds for bedding the plank laps, and usually more attention is paid to this.

Strip-planked boats are built of narrow strips, usually of cedar. These strips are fastened edge to edge to give virtually a one-piece, round-bottomed shell. A well-built model will have the edges of its strips shaped concave and convex, bedded in a suitable compound, and edge-fastened at close intervals.

It's a rather common practice to treat the hull with a wood preservative. This not only guards against rot, but also reduces contraction and expansion of the wood, making for less likelihood of seams opening.

Despite the precautions taken in building, it's possible for a strip-planked boat to leak in trailer service, especially in a hot-and-dry climate. Storing the boat in the shade is sensible, as is painting it white to reflect heat. Some manufacturers offer fiberglassed models which, of course, remain leak-free.

Fiberglass is particularly adaptable to molded shapes. Foam flotation overcomes weight handicap, adds stability.

Whatever type of wood boat you're considering, there's one point you should keep in mind. For salt water, the fastenings shouldn't be susceptible to rusting or corrosion. The better-built wood boats usually have bronze or brass fasteners.

FIBERGLASS BOATS

With fiberglass boats, more so than with those of other constructions, quality—or the lack of it—is largely a hidden feature. In fact, your only real measure of a glass boat's worth is the reputation and know-how of its manufacturer.

One of the advantages of using fiberglass is its adaptability to forming compound or two-way curves. A shapely round-bottomed hull is almost as easy to produce as a flat one. Even multicurved surfaces and unusual surface effects are possible. This advantage has been responsible for a great improvement in boat design, particularly in outboard boats. Resulting hulls have pleasing lines and superior performance characteristics.

Unfortunately, though, this very adaptability of fiberglass also made it possible to produce craft of freakish design. Often they perform indifferently and soon become dated in appearance. However, the selection of a design is entirely up to the buyer. Each of us has his own ideas of what a boat should look like. What counts is how the boat will perform—how fast it is, how seaworthy and safe, how comfortable, and how it steers and handles.

Great strides have been made in the finishing of glass boats. Nowadays you see some lovely molding jobs, with the outside surfaces glasslike and the inner surfaces smooth. There's no longer any excuse for inner surfaces to be rough, uneven, or show areas that are bare of resin.

The general practice is to apply what's called a gel coat to the female mold. This gel coat, which becomes the exterior surface, is a heavy layer of resin in which pigments may be mixed to produce molded-in color. Unfortunately, these molded-in colors have some tendency to fade. Even so, such a surface has a greater lasting quality with more resistance to wear and abrasion than has ordinary paint.

If your fiberglass boat does fade or discolor objectionably—or you merely want a different color scheme—you can, of course, paint it. Paint manufacturers have developed special techniques for fiberglass craft, the important product being a special primer intended to give the paint itself proper adherence to the hard surface.

Fiberglass boats are proof against salt-water worms. Yet most owners—where a boat is left in salt water for lengthy periods—prefer to use an antifouling or bottom paint designed to resist the attachment of grass, shells, and so on. If an unprotected bottom is allowed to collect scum and barnacles, the harsh scraping required to remove the encrusted growth won't help the fiberglass surface.

Despite the many advantages of making boats of fiberglass, there are two disadvantages which manufacturers face: weight and price. There's also one lesser objection to this material—because its density is greater than that of water, the boat would sink if swamped unless precautions were taken. Manufacturers find it easy and relatively inexpensive to get around this difficulty. Ordinarily, it's done by incorporating blocks of some flotation material. One way is to use the so-called foaming material that adheres to the fiberglass laminate. Another is to trap air within structural members or between double bottoms. The better manufacturers are careful to provide flotation well in excess of the boat's maximum requirements.

ALUMINUM BOATS

Of all the metal boats produced today, possibly 99 percent are aluminum. And aluminum is a prime contender with wood and fiberglass as a boat-building material.

Aluminum boats are bought mainly by people who demand low-cost, lightweight purely utilitarian craft. As the records show, aluminum's very popular with fishermen. Boat-livery operators appreciate its durability and attractive cost, and aluminum canoes outsell all others.

It's true that you can now get larger, faster aluminum boats, including sport runabouts and lavishly fitted-out cruisers. One of the big reasons is that recent developments in alloys have made advanced styling much easier.

Still, it's in the small and medium-size brackets that aluminum boats have gained their greatest popularity—prams, dinghies, skiffs, auto-toppers, canoes, plain runabouts, and utilities.

Aluminum by itself would be a very weak metal for boat building. So the general practice has been to combine—alloy—other metals with it.

Gradually but constantly, better aluminum alloys have been developed, and they in turn have permitted better ways of building boats.

Alloy designations can be very confusing to the layman. So long as you're dealing with a reputable manufacturer, it's sensible to assume that he's used what's proper for the particular type and size of boat involved.

Unless you have a good reason for wanting an ultralight craft, it's sensible to buy one that's reasonably heavy for its type and size. You can logically assume that a heavier boat will be more durable.

Aluminum, in sheet form, lends itself well to the production of simple hull forms such as flat-bottomed prams and skiffs, and even straight-sectioned craft with semi-V bottoms.

Welded ⅛-inch aluminum plate permits complex hull shapes like this multihull runabout.

Joining the parts of the hull together is a critical operation in boatbuilding. The majority of the builders depend upon rivets. The rivets on some early boats caused trouble, but manufacturers now avoid this by using rivets with the same corrosion and temper qualities as the sheets used on the hull.

In some of the more expensive aluminum hulls, heavier material and welded seams are successfully used.

If the boat is to be sold as a natural-finish model, buffing and polishing will finish it. But if it's to be painted, a special preparatory treatment, called anodizing, is given it.

Good progress has been made in developing special finish treatments.

One manufacturer, for instance, bonds vinyl plastic to the aluminum, providing a finish that's good looking and is claimed to be exceptionally durable.

Boats that will be constantly used in salt water require bottom protection against barnacles and other growths. A special bottom paint that will do this job is now available and can be applied at the factory or by the boat owner. This paint is nonmetallic, so it has no harmful galvanic action on the aluminum. Often the exposed inner surfaces of the hull will be given a special protective treatment, making them skid-proof and giving a sound-deadening effect.

A heavier, larger boat will not be noticeably noisy. Aluminum itself is a "dead" metal giving off a dull sound—not the sharp one of steel. Besides, reinforcing members tend to quiet the hull, and plastic foam used as flotation material has sound-deadening qualities. This type of flotation material also avoids those popping sounds that an older boat, with its built-in safety air chambers, could give off as the temperature changes.

If you've been used to canvas-covered canoes, you'll find an aluminum one not as quiet. Still, there's no denying that metal canoes have proved superior for hard, wilderness use.

In duck hunting, where you encounter thin ice, a light aluminum boat can be noisy. On the other hand, you don't have to worry about the boat being cut by the ice.

An aluminum boat, they claim, can be as nearly maintenance-free as any boat you can find. In salt water, however, even though the boat is designed for such use, an occasional hosing off is good practice.

You can paint your natural-finish aluminum boat, of course, but to do it right requires special treatment with special products. You can get everything you need for the job from any major manufacturer of marine finishes. And while the job of repainting a painted boat is ordinarily easy, it's wise in this day of special finishes to make absolutely certain that what you're using will be entirely compatible with the finish that was put on originally.

An aluminum boat will take a lot of punishment. And though it may get battered, most likely it will still be in perfectly reliable condition. Dents can be tapped flush. Punctures—which in a good boat are so unlikely its manufacturer may guarantee against them—can be repaired.

Small aluminum boats and canoes are light for their strength and size, so they're fine for carrying on a car and for portaging; in the larger sizes, they're very convenient to use with a trailer.

In addition to their light weight, low-cost maintenance, and built-in quality features, aluminum craft generally are attractively priced.

2 Flat-Bottomed Boats

(PRAMS, PUNTS & JOHNBOATS)

IF ALL of the boats with flat bottoms and flat ends were tied bow to stern, surely they would extend the length of the Mississippi River and you could step from one to another all of the way from St. Paul to New Orleans and never get your feet wet.

This statement won't have the blessing of spokesmen for the boating industry who use some manufacturers' production figures and some state boating registrations to come up with creditable estimates of the number of boats in use. But, allowing for the fact that many boats because of small size and clandestine birth are never recorded, we'll go out on a stout yardarm and offer this as an unofficial observation.

Punts, prams and johnboats belong to this prolific family, and their family resemblance is a dead giveaway—they all are flat on the bottom and square at each end. They are the simplest boats to build, responding well to rough lumber, little skill and few tools. What is important in this day of precut-standardization, they can be assembled from stock sheets and scraps of readily available plywood. This means you can build one in your backyard or buy one tailor-made for the contents of a small piggy bank. In going one step beyond the hollowed log, these boats do have frames, but only a bare minimum of them and they depend on their seats to act as braces.

Often the doughty pram is a boy's first ship, frequently it is dressed up and serves as tender for imposing yachts. At their best, the refined versions are quite amenable to simple sails, outboard motors of low horsepower and good old Swedish steam—the dependable oar.

In longer versions, you will find them as narrow punts poled by watermen through twisting rivers of marsh country. (If the ends are pointed, it's a bateau.) A little broader of beam and it will be called a johnboat—a dependable workhorse that can be coaxed across river sandbars even when heavily laden with camping gear.

The rugged johnboat is perhaps the sportsman's most valuable aid. This favorite of the Mississippi River and its tributaries has retained its appeal for many years, and it has an impressive record of usefulness among hunters, trappers, and fishermen. Modern versions of the johnboat are

This excellent example of a pram is 7'9" and weighs only 79 pounds. Plans for its construction are available for 25¢ from the American Plywood Association, 1119 A St., Tacoma, Washington 98401.

A flat-bottomed, square-ended johnboat is a good shallow-water fishing craft.

Lightweight, aluminum johnboat is easy to launch and haul out.

greatly improved over the old ones, but the basic hull shape has remained virtually unchanged from early times.

Johnboats are utiltarian craft, and as such they well serve the purposes of sport fishermen. The fact that the boats are shaped like scows, square at the bow as well as the stern, has many advantages. For one thing, it gives the boats a great load-carrying capacity. The square bow provides a lot of usable space up forward. Moreover, the bow can be beached end-on to afford a firm footing when loading and unloading occupants and their gear.

The flat bottom with its rising curve forward makes the johnboat unusually convenient to handle out of water. It can be hauled on the simplest sort of trailer, and may be carried in back of a small truck or station wagon. Short hauls can even be made on rollers. We've seen large johnboats hitched behind cars and dragged short distances over forest trails and dirt roads.

Such harsh treatment, plus knocking about among rocks and snags in shallow water, are in keeping with johnboat service, and the boats are made to take it. Most wood johnboats have their bottoms protected with several hardwood longitudinals, and the better-made aluminum ones are protected by a series of bottom extrusions.

The basic simplicity of johnboats makes them easy to build. This undoubtedly played an important part in their early development and is now contributing to a renewal of interest in them. This ease-of-construction feature, however, has had its negative aspects. Over the years, it has resulted in the production of some poorly built boats, and this has given rise to a tendency to regard johnboats generally as crude, heavy, clumsy, hard to row or paddle, and slow when powered by a motor.

Well-built johnboats, and other types of craft that have evolved from them, are not clumsy or hard to handle. They could be the best choice of craft for use on rivers and small inland waters. The fact that more and more dealers are now handling lines of johnboats reflects a general awareness and appreciation of the craft's good qualities.

The square ends and flat bottoms of the johnboat lend themselves to economical production in all materials—wood, plywood, fiberglass, steel, and aluminum. Aluminum is now the most widely favored commercial form of construction for these boats. Wood and plywood boats, however, are still favored by amateur builders, and many outfitters who offer float trips on rivers prefer wood for their 20-foot and longer johnboats.

The craft's simplicity makes building a johnboat out of wood a practical spare-time project. If you should be inclined to try it, get yourself a good set of plans. Good plans should provide for specific hull characteristics. For example, the boat's sides and ends should not be perpendicular; they should have some flare outward. Though the bottom should be flat from side to side, it also should have some rocker fore and aft. Toward the bow, the bottom should sweep upward, and the same goes for the gunwales. These features avoid giving the boat a boxy appearance.

The boat's beam should be on the narrow side, approaching about one

This 16-foot aluminum johnboat, weighing only 250 pounds, can handle outboard motors up to 30 h.p. With a good pair of oars, it can be rowed for fishing.

fourth the length. This ratio works out best in 14 and 16-foot hulls. Boats shorter than that and especially those under 12 feet, tend to be more of the pram type and do not have the advantages of the true johnboat.

It took the use of aluminum by manufacturers to make johnboats nationally popular in both the pleasure and work-boat fields. The availability of more suitable alloys has helped. An efficient manufacturer can produce an aluminum johnboat at comparatively low cost, and by shipping them nested can keep transportation costs down. Competition in this field helps to keep consumer prices fairly low even though many extra features such as live-bait wells are often built into these boats.

A typical factory-produced boat intended for the sportsman should not be unduly light. A good 14-foot model is likely to weigh around 150 pounds, a 16-footer close to 250. The heavier plating, the number and size of supporting members, and the built-in features all tend to increase the weight. In some 16-footers, the forward seat is virtually a sunken deck similar to those in many expensive, specially built, open fishing boats. Other seats, in addition to acting as stiffening members and serving as containers for flotation material, are likely to have built-in features such as live-bait wells, ice chests, and tackle boxes. Integral keels improve the boat's performance and also make for greater rigidity. The transom structure is likely to be on the massive side.

Heavier, larger johnboats are usually fast, but they don't behave badly at low speeds or with a small motor. A typical 14-footer with a 6-h.p. motor should do about 14 m.p.h. With two people aboard, speed should be about 12 m.p.h. With a 10-h.p. motor, speed should be around 23 m.p.h. with one person, and close to 20 m.p.h. with two aboard. The same boat in a 16 feet, with a 20-h.p. motor, should do nearly 30 m.p.h. Properly designed, these boats will also handle nicely at slow and trolling speeds. With a decent pair of oars and lightly loaded, either boat should row well enough for fishing.

The larger boat would be ideal for weekend cruising and camping. It would take two persons and considerable gear. Filled with a home-made

19

Big 18-footer is quite roomy even with three or four aboard. Cabin is usually demountable.

shelter of some sort, and equipped with air mattresses and sleeping bags, it could even be used for sleeping aboard. A 10-h.p. motor would suffice for such use and would be economical on all-day runs. Because of the boat's shallow draft and husky bottom, you could explore or fish shallow streams.

If you are interested in camping trips by boat, there are modifications of the johnboat which afford advantages of a sizable cabin and a long forward deck. Some of them are quite large, but even on an 18-footer with a beam of about 6½ feet, there's a lot of living and storage space. Yet, this type of johnboat draws much less water than most other boats of comparable size. In aluminum, an 18-footer with a cabin weighs approximately 600 pounds, and that's not much considering the carrying capacity. Using a 35-h.p. motor and with one couple and their gear aboard, speed should be about 25 m.p.h.

The next step up would be a scow-type houseboat in a size small enough to be trailerable. Power could be an outboard motor or a small inboard with a stern drive. A good example of this type, 18 feet 9 inches long and with a beam of 7 feet 3 inches, affords roomy living and sleeping quarters for two persons.

Another modification of the johnboat is known as the garvey. It is built and used principally along the New Jersey coast. This boat is little appreciated except in its native habitat. While most garveys are inboards, stern-drive powering would be entirely satisfactory. Garveys are shallow-draft boats, but the propeller is well protected, and this makes them ideal for use in shoal water. Yet, a garvey's bulk and weight often allow its use under conditions which keep smaller and lighter boats in the harbor.

The garvey has a johnboat's characteristics and many of its advantages, but a lot of refining has been done to develop the basic hull form for open-water conditions. A garvey has a blunt bow, but the sides are high enough to raise it well above the water. The sides are flared and the sheer or gunwale shows a pleasing curve as in a well-designed johnboat. The bottom, however, has more shape. It's flat in the middle of the boat, but some V-shape is

20

worked in where the bottom curves upward to the bow. Astern, the center of the garvey's bottom rises sharply, but the chines—the joining of the bottom and sides—are both carried almost straight back and they're lower than the centerline. This results in an inverted, V-shaped tunnel which affords the propeller good protection.

Even in 20-foot and longer garveys, the hull remains simple enough for easy and economical building. Garveys are usually plainly furnished. Small builders along the New Jersey coast turn these boats out at remarkably low cost. Each builder has his own ideas about shape and construction based on what has proved best along his particular stretch of coast. Unfortunately, one can seldom order a garvey by mail. First, you scout out a builder and then buy or order in person.

Garvey, popular on New Jersey coast, resembles johnboat but usually has inboard.

3 Selecting a Canoe

FOR MANY OF US, there isn't a boat afloat that can conjure the romance of a canoe. It is one of the earliest craft, long known in many parts of the world, usually in the form of a log hollowed by burning and scraping. None, however, quite reached the zenith attained by the North American Indians with their birchbark canoes—light enough to be easily carried by one man, but strong enough to carry many times his weight.

Obviously our materials and building methods have improved, but not the beautiful and efficient design. And today, canoes are putting a sense of conquest back into the outdoors. Probably this, more than anything else, is responsible for the recent revival of interest in them. A canoe can put you closer to woods and water than any other type of craft. More and more sportsmen are finding that small creeks and streams near their homes, waters too shallow for conventional boats, can be fished and explored by canoe. Many rivers have deep potholes in isolated upper stretches, and the angler who doesn't mind manhandling a canoe over fallen trees and similar obstacles will generally find good fishing in such areas. Campers who rely on canoes for transportation find attractive campsites plentiful, which is not the case with car campers limited to road travel.

Another big factor contributing to their growing popularity has been the great increase in the number of places renting canoes. Liveries racking up to 100 canoes are becoming commonplace. Many rental places now store customers' canoes. What also has helped is the willingness of liveries to provide instruction for novices. All this has given impetus to the desire for canoe ownership.

The current availability and attractive pricing of canoe kits is stimulating a lot of interest in these craft. Otherwise, one can choose from the offerings of over fifty manufacturers. Square-stern models as well as the conventional can be had, and most lines offer at least the popular sizes.

About thirty manufacturers produce fiberglass canoes, sand possibly twenty offer aluminum ones. There are also molded plywood and panel types and a fair choice of canvas-covered models. A newcomer is a type molded of rubberlike material. The shell, 3/8-inches thick, has a center layer of foam between inner and outer layers of a hard rubber, said to be resistant to oil, acids, and such, and easily repairable. Weight for a 16-footer is 70 pounds.

Canadian builders are competing more actively for U.S. business, notably in the canvas-covered and cedar-strip types. Fortunately, apart from small refinements, no serious attempts are being made to improve on the traditional shapes.

Kayaks, both the quality folding makes and even the rigids, are of interest to paddlers who want more action than a canoe may provide. And collapsible canvas boats and canoes, along with other offerings designed to fold flat, have widened the choice for sportsmen who want compactness as well as light weight.

Buying a canoe can be easy or difficult, depending on what you want and how easily you're satisfied. The canoe-buying situation is unusual since it's difficult to get a complete picture of what the market has to offer.

Shopping for a canoe among local boat dealers presents a problem. Most stock only a single make in a popular size and type. If you're easily satisfied, it's likely some local dealer could fit you out with a more or less standard canoe. But if you're not easily satisfied, you'll be hard put to find a dealer who carries a fair assortment of models and sizes in stock or who can help you order a canoe from listings in catalogs.

How can you beat this situation? First, check on all the boat dealers in your area. If you're lucky, you may find one who stocks a variety of models or who can and will order the particular model you want. Second, if you can't find such a dealer, compile a file of literature on canoes by writing to manufacturers. Fortunately, all the makers will sell direct if they're unable to refer you to a local representative.

Regardless of how you shop for a canoe, you may be confused by the variety of constructions and types now available. But you won't go far astray if you buy from a well-known, reputable manufacturer and are willing to pay a fair price.

Choice of construction has become largely a matter of personal preference. Asking the advice of several canoe owners, each with a different type, may only confuse you, for each most likely will favor his own craft and possibly be ignorant or misinformed about other types. The man who owns a relatively new canvas-covered canoe will stress the improvements that have been made in such craft, such as plastic coverings highly resistant to damage and easily repaired. The man with an aluminum boat will boast how it has stood up to harsh usage and needs a minimum of maintenance. If you have saltwater service in mind, he'll tell you about the treatments used in factory painting that protect the alloy against corrosion. The owner of a fiberglass canoe will tell you about the ease of upkeep, and how manufacturers have licked the old problem of providing strength in the long, slim hull while still keeping the weight down. The owner of a new molded-plywood rig, will proudly show his canoe's superb varnished-mahogany finish. And if you object to its being easily marred or the finish being too difficult to maintain, he'll counter by saying that ordering a model in painted finish could be the answer. Whatever you may be told, the important point to remember is that all these constructions have now reached a high point of quality.

Keen competition among manufacturers, as well as among trade groups backing the different materials, keeps prices pretty much in line. Canoes have always been relatively expensive, and the use of new materials or techniques hasn't changed the situation. As it is, from $250 to $300 for 17-foot canoes, regardless of construction, seems the price range when sold through dealers. Weights for the various types are also competitive, from 75 to 85 pounds being the usual range for this popular size.

Another type still very much in the picture so far as outdoorsmen are concerned is the folding canvas canoe. While conventional canoes can be considered portable, the covered-framework folding type has the added advantage of compactness in that it can be collapsed and carried in a bag. We'll cover them in greater detail in another chapter.

Sponson canoes, with their bulky side chambers providing extra flotation, are largely off the market. The wood in a canvas-covered canoe will float if it capsizes, and aluminum and fiberglass canoes have either air chambers or synthetic floatation material as a safeguard against sinking. Also available are special pontoons or side floats. These detachable pontoons are designed to make a canoe capsize-resistant, as well as to steady it for fishing, shooting, and when used with an outboard motor.

Panel plywood permits kit manufacturers to offer ready-cut parts for chinetype canoes. There's even a range of lengths in both square-stern and regular models. Some other kit manufacturers supply complete requirements for assembling the rigid, covered-framework type. Kit prices run from $25 to around $100. Plans are also available for building your own canoe, but construction is difficult. What model and size canoe should you buy? The first thing to decide is whether you'll want to use a motor, and, if so, to what extent you'll use it. A motor takes much of the hard work out of canoeing, but if you rely on it too much you'll deprive yourself of much of the enjoyment of canoe ownership. Any standard 16- or 17-foot canoe should take a motor up to 3h.p. mounted on a bracket to one side of the stern. Use a larger motor and, instead of increasing the speed, you'll make the canoe tricky to handle and unsafe. The conventional canoe's sharp stern is unsuited for more power and this, coupled with the off-center mounting of the motor, is dangerous from the standpoint of stability.

If you expect to use a motor more than a paddle, and particularly if you're interested in speed, a square-stern canoe might be a better choice. Some square-sterns are extreme, being virtually outboards. Others are true canoes, with the bottom sharpness at the stern largely preserved while providing a narrow and rather high transom for the motor. The wider the stern, the more efficiently the power will be utilized. However, paddling performance will be sacrificed in proportion to the width of the stern. Because of such variances in stern shapes, no set rule applies for powering square-stern canoes. Just play safe by keeping well within the manufacturer's horsepower recommendation for the model.

The sensible approach when choosing a square-stern canoe is to aim for

Pontoons make this square-stern canoe steady and capsize-resistant.

Canoe drives well with 3 h.p. outboard. Larger motors on side mounts are unsafe.

This fork device, common in the South, protects prop in weed-infested waters.

a model that will paddle well and still have a transom that will take a minimum-size motor more efficiently than a conventional canoe of matching size. Even then, you may have to make allowances for the motor on the stern. Your weight aft, plus that of the motor, could cause broken water to come in over the stern occasionally. One answer to this would be to put the heavier passenger or any added weight forward. When fishing with the motor off but left on the stern, it's common for one or two anglers to keep their weight forward, paddling stern first with the transom and raised motor clear of the water.

Typical of the square-sterned models which can be powered by an outboard motor is this one in aluminum by Grumman. Note the splash keels.

There should be no question about the actual model or hull shape itself. The so-called guide's model is by far the most practical. The characteristics are rather straight gunwales with ends low, beam carried well into the ends, the bottom rather flat although rounded into the sides, and the keel shod with a strip and quite straight except for some rockering at the ends. The guide's model is a good load-carrier that paddles easily and holds its course well. Avoid a canoe with a narrow beam or a bottom that is too rounded; it will be tippy and will not carry weight well. Also avoid high ends; the wind will use them as sails and make the craft cranky to handle.

For the beginning canoeist, size should be his big concern. The secret of easy paddling is having a canoe that is the right size for the load ordinarily carried. A 17-footer, for example, will paddle easier than a 16-foot model if the weight of its occupants and gear would put the 16-footer deep in the water. Not less than 6 inches of freeboard, when loaded for fairly smooth water, and more when the going is rough, is a sensible rule for good handling and safety. This means that even for a lengthy cruise, a 17-footer will carry two persons, a camping outfit, and up to a three-weeks supply of food. Or a 16-

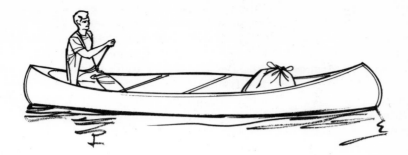

A lone canoeist trims his craft by equalizing his weight with his camping equipment.

footer will take two persons with a light outfit and food enough for a trip where supplies for easily replenishable along the way. The 17-footer would also be better suited for fairly open waters. Where portaging or car-carrying is involved, the extra weight of a 17-footer over a 16-foot model, around 10 pounds, wouldn't be objectionable. It's for these reasons that 17-footers are becoming the most popular size for general use.

Smaller canoes as well as larger ones are available, of course. Canoes of 18 and 20 feet are in common use for wilderness trips where heavy loads must be carried. But where the number of persons in the party is a consideration, it is better to use two ordinary-size canoes, each loaded with its own outfit, rather than a single large craft.

The practical minimum-size for a canoe is 11 feet. A good size for one paddler is 12 to 13 feet, for two paddlers 15 feet. Although 15-foot models may weigh only about 50 pounds, they are roomy for their length. They tend to be stubby and full-beamed, usually 35 inches or even wider, and a good 12

This 15-foot model, a 50-pounder, is fine for narrow, confined streams.

inches deep, which is equal to the standard 16 and 17-foot canoes. These smaller canoes are often called trapper's canoes or hunting canoes, and they're fine for one-day trips on narrow, confined streams. Their shortness and light weight also make them ideal for fishing waters that can only be reached by portaging.

Be a crank when buying paddles. Good ones aren't easy to find. A proper paddle will have that fine quality of feeling right, and it will be a joy to use. Eventually, worthwhile paddles of synthetic materials will be produced, but until they are, those made of spruce, maple, and ash are the best. Canoe manufacturers, especially the old-established builders, are your best bet for quality paddles. Even though you may have the best of paddles, it's wise to carry a spare.

Regardless of quality, a canoe paddle will never feel quite right unless it's the correct length and shape for the paddler. The traditional length rule is that the paddle should be 3 inches under your height for stern work and 6 inches under your height for bow paddling.

Canoe equipment should be kept to a minimum. You'll need a bailer, and a large sponge. Also carry an emergency repair kit suitable for the construction of your canoe. Add a couple of life-preserver cushions and you've got the basic equipment for short trips. When paddling, it's best to kneel on one, bracing against a thwart.

Other equipment can be added as needed. Suitable side mounts or brackets for small outboard motors, as well as carrying yokes for portaging, are available. Some yokes, incidentally, are now being molded in fiberglass and are trim, lightweight, and easy to stow. If you intend to use your canoe for float-fishing or jump-shooting, you should carry a foot or so of heavy chain to attach to a long line for use as a drag to slow your drift in a swift current. The line could be a 50-foot length of 1/4-inch nylon or 3/8-inch manila, which you could also use to tow your canoe up a turbulent stretch by walking along the bank.

4 Dories

THERE ARE more misconceptions about the dory than any other type of craft. Generally, these impressions are the result of the glamour and history attached to the dory. It's easy to be influenced by what you have read of the craft's amazing behavior in rough water. Another factor which often confuses boatmen is the great number of types of craft called dory-built boats. Each of these types, however, has some advantage over the original dory design, and a prospective buyer should not disregard these modified dories, since one of them is almost sure to fill his needs far better than a true dory.

Let's trace, with the help of the accompanying sketches, the evolution of the dory to the present-day modifications of this craft, most of which are better boats than the original dory and more suitable for modern boat-building materials and construction methods.

The traditional Banks dory, also known as the Banker or Gloucester dory, is the model on which the reputation of dories was founded. It is a lean, straight-sided, nearly double-ended true dory with crescent sheer, flared sides, and a tombstone stern. The Banks dory is the renowned work boat of the codfishermen on the Grand Banks of Newfoundland. During the late 1800's and well into this century, fishermen used these dories when working out from the mother schooner in tending their trawls or long lines of baited hooks, usually in all but the worst winter weather. All too often, a fisherman and his mate got lost in the fog or snow for days and sometimes weeks, surviving only because of their dory's seaworthiness and, of course, their own heartiness and seamanship. A dory was even sailed single-handed across the Atlantic.

In the days of commercial sailing, when Gloucester, Massachusetts, was still the first fishing port of the world, thousands of new dories were built each year to replace those worn out or smashed or swept overboard from vessels in storms. A single New England town, toward the close of the century, had ten separate boat-building establishments turning out dories. They were even shipped cross-country for the Alaskan fisheries on canvas-covered flat-cars called ghost trains in New England. In Alaska, as well as on the East Coast, the dory has had a decided effect on small-boat design over the years.

Canada's Maritime Provinces were big producers of dories, too. Production was efficiently organized, usually on a piecework basis, using templates or patterns and even precut parts. Sizes ran from 12 to 16 feet, using the old method of bottom measurement, meaning respectively 16 to 20 feet in over-all length. The going price, as late as just before World War II was $1 a foot.

With the eventual replacement of dory trawls by motorized dragging, the dory gradually lost out. Even so, because of their inherent seaworthiness, durability, and low cost, dories which are practically counterparts of those of the 80's are still carried by commercial craft for survival purposes if not for regular use. One practical feature of dories that's still a big plus today is that the thwarts can be removed and the boats nested within one another, though this was much more of an advantage in the days when a schooner carried her load of dories on deck. Various government agencies and beach associations also continue to favor the true dory for rescue service, particularly where a rescue may involve passing through or working in the surf.

Don't let yourself be carried away by the glamorous aspects of the true dory. They have their disadvantages, and these are likely to show up badly in pleasure service. The disadvantages hinge on two related points: the fact that the dory was designed as a work boat, and its distinctive type of construction. So far as the shape is concerned, no actual improvement has been made. Dory construction starts with a flat bottom of wide, heavy boards cleated together and cut to shape on the outside edges. The design of the bottom determines the shape of the finished hull. Bend and fasten wide-board sides around the bottom and the dory is essentially built.

Understandably, the result is a heavy boat. And, as with all ordinary wood boats, the dory will leak after launching if it has been out of the water for some time. Both these faults are at their worst in today's trend toward trailering. Though easy to row for a boat of such size and weight, a dory calls for plenty of rowing beef. While extremely able and capable of carrying heavy loads, the dory is a tricky craft to board, climb out of, and move about in.

Buying a dory nowadays requires hunting out a builder familiar with the design. On the other hand, if you want to build your own, there's a good choice of plans. But building such a boat is not as simple as you might assume from the preceding description of dory construction. The side planking is difficult. Forming the odd shapes required and fitting and fastening the planks lapstrake fashion are not easy jobs.

Thanks to modern materials and boat-building products, dories are now available which embody the attractive features of the true dory, but largely avoid its faults. The modern adaptation shown in the sketches is a 15½-footer of plywood-plastic construction. It weighs 125 pounds, which is about half what a small dory of conventional construction would weigh. This light weight, along with the dory characteristics being retained produces a seaworthy boat that is a pleasure to row. The fact that this modern adaptation is of leakproof construction is also important, since such a boat is likely to be kept out of the water and launched off the beach, or possibly trailered. Even the price, roughly $200, compares favorably with what you might spend to have a conventional dory built to order.

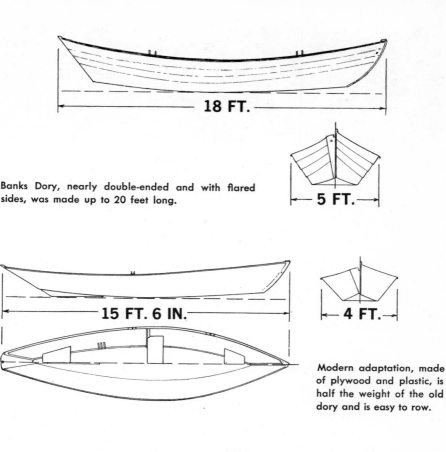

18 FT.

5 FT.

Banks Dory, nearly double-ended and with flared sides, was made up to 20 feet long.

15 FT. 6 IN.

4 FT.

Modern adaptation, made of plywood and plastic, is half the weight of the old dory and is easy to row.

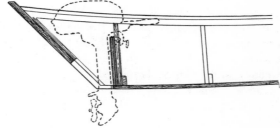

This Gardner-type installation provides a watertight motor well at dory's stern.

However, this modern adaptation and the conventional dory, being designed for easy rowing, make poor powerboats. The high, deep-V transom requires a long-shaft motor, if not a special mount or bracket. Also, because of the hull's length and narrowness and its tendency to lift easily over wave crests, the motor's propeller occasionally will come out of the water and race madly. To avoid these faults, it is common practice to install a motor well. either of the types shown in the sketches puts the motor into the boat where engine weight is lower and better placed for greater efficiency. Even so, you should avoid overpowering. The sharp-stern characteristic of the dory makes

This 22-footer, a modern version of New England dory, has semi-rounded bottom.

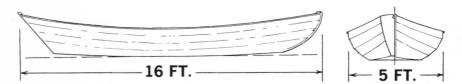

|← 16 FT. →| |← 5 FT. →|

Swampscott dory featured rounded sides, fuller transom. This is a rowing model. Drawing at right shows bow and stern views.

for easy rowing and excellent behavior in a following sea, but, from the power or speed standpoint, the lack of bottom bearing aft is bad.

The Swampscott dory was originally developed as an improvement on the traditional Banks dory. The chief difference is in the knuckled, rounded sides. Another modification, which showed up as outboard motors appeared, was a gradual widening of the transom. The rounded sides produced more boat, and more initial stability, for the given length. This change also permitted the retention of dory performance in a boat of shorter length. One thing that can't be done in modifying the true dory is to scale the boat down proportionately. That is, you cannot decrease beam, depth, and length in the same ratio and still have a safe and seaworthy boat.

The Swampscott dory, with either a narrow tombstone transom or a slightly fuller stern, lends itself well to ultralight construction. As far back as the 80's, batten-seam construction was used to provide dories which were very light and even stronger than those of heavy conventional construction. Later, with the advent of waterproof plywood, 14-footers weighing as little as 65 pounds were produced. More recently, big 18-footers with 1/4-inch plywood on battens let into side frames and finally covered with Dynel (a polypropylene fabric) have been built to weigh around 200 pounds, about one-third lighter than a dory of conventional construction.

The semidory outboard is the result of an effort to retain the characteristics of the Swampscott type but provide a boat capable of keeping up with the continuous increase of outboard horsepower. The semidory is a highly practical fishing boat. In fact, versions of it remain the most popular of the

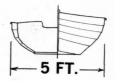

Semidory outboard has old dory features and a wide transom for outboard power.

all-wood boats offered by manufacturers. Though low or reasonably priced, the better offerings reflect the use of modern boat-building materials. By using plywood for the shaped strakes of planking and bedding their laps with a proper sealer, possibly covering with fiberglass or Dynel, an amateur builder can produce a light, strong boat that will remain tight.

The Flatiron outboard in its present-day form, with its wide bottom and full stern, shows dory characteristics in the rather high bow with slanted stem. Its chief appeal is to the manufacturer aiming at the low-price market and, similarly, to the amateur builder who wants to use plywood for an easily built improvement over the ordinary flat-bottomed skiff.

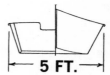

Flatiron dory, the best bet for amateur builders, has a wide bottom, full stern.

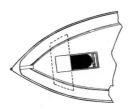

Pacific Coast double-ender embodies old dory characteristics in a big boat. Note the inside well for outboard motor.

The Pacific Coast double-ender and the dory-type day cruiser are good examples of what has been done to embody the chief characteristics of the dory in big boats. The Pacific Coast dory, being a double-ender, is a seaworthy craft. The plywood construction is smooth and lends itself well to fiberglassing. These boats, 20 feet long or shorter, are used by both commercial and sport fishermen, particularly along the upper coast, for salmon or sea bass fishing. This calls for use of a trailer, since the boat must first be pulled down to the surf behind a protecting promontory. The actual trip through the surf is made under oar power. After this, when well beyond the inshore breakers,

Dory day cruiser can be adapted for either outboard or inboard-outboard power.

the outboard motor is started and the fisherman is all set for a day of deep-sea fishing. The motor well makes using a motor under rough water conditions far safer and more efficient than it would be with a side-bracket mount. Though most are built locally on the West Coast, the availability of building plans for these double-enders, in cabin models as well as open boats, has resulted in a growing number of similar dories appearing in the East.

The square-stern, cabin dory cruiser is another example of what clever designing can do to modify the dory for present-day use. For this general type, building plans can be had in a range of hull sizes and superstructure arrangements.

Additional proof of the far-reaching effects of the dory on modern design is that one of the biggest builders of boats in the country—Chris Craft—builds two contemporary 22-foot versions of the famous old New England dories. We have a hunch boat manufacturers generally will make a greater effort to cater to the growing number of men who take fishing seriously enough to want a boat specially designed for their sport.

5 Utilities and Runabouts

UTILITY, according to Mr. Webster, is a quality or state of being useful —an apt, though unflattering, term for the unpretentious type of boat seen on all waterways. It is claimed by no area as its brainchild. It's just a plain boat, the least complicated, the least sophisticated, requiring the least upkeep —and yet it is the closest approach to an all-purpose boat. It's the common type found at resort lakes and in rental fleets—fairly easy to tow, to row, or to propel by just about any size outboard motor.

This boat is the best choice if you just want to get someplace; or if you just want to fish (most boatmen do, sooner or later); or if you require only a seat, some leg room, and a whole world of headroom; or if you want uncomplicated operation.

We're discussing the utility: the fisherman's workhorse.

Dress the same boat up a bit with the bow decked over, a windshield, steering wheel and instrument panel, and you have a runabout. This is the model which has an element of familiarity for the fugitive from the highways. In fact, for a brief unlamented period some boatbuilders seemed to copy all of the worst of Detroit's highway products to dress this boat up—tail fins, chrome doodads, and the mixed-tone color schemes of a bathroom in a flashy motel. Fortunately, that trend was short-lived.

A small, inexpensive utility may best suit your purposes. The plainly finished model is often the sensible choice. It will be priced less than the fancier runabout which may be your first preference. It will also require less maintenance, less effort, and less money to preserve its appearance and condition. Not being of extreme design, it will not become dated nor will it lose its trade-in value nearly as quickly as a highly stylized one. Because less power and consequently less fuel is required, cost of operation will be more modest. Gasoline and oil represent the continuing expense of operating a powerboat, and a big outboard motor has a healthy appetite for both. In a fisherman's service, a big motor is likely to be used mainly for getting to and from the fishing grounds. For trolling and short runs, it's becoming common practice to use a small motor carried aboard for the purpose.

You can expect to pay $500 and up for a good small utility and a small motor. Double the price for a runabout of the same size, material, and configuration. You can expect the cost of upkeep to become noticeable with a runabout because its style usually calls for materials and trim requiring varnish or polish or both.

BOATS FOR SHELTERED WATERS

If your use of a boat will be limited to protected waters, your requirements are relatively simple and your investment can be quite low. For sheltered waters, such as ponds, small lakes, and small rivers, you don't want a large or heavy boat. These waterways are likely to be narrow, winding, shallow in places, and possibly obstructed by rocks, sandbars, or fallen trees. Since any body of sheltered water will afford only a limited amount of running, it's best to be equipped for maximum portability. The boat for this service should be one that can be man-handled when necessary. Quite often you may have to park some distance from the water and lug your boat to it.

In smaller sizes you have maximum mobility; the boats are easy to row and require only a small motor. Larger models will be drier and more comfortable but they scarifice mobility—they are not easy to tote and they are not easy to row.

A boat for these ideal conditions should not be over 12 feet long, nor should it weigh over 100 pounds. It should be a bare boat without extras to increase weight. You may want to carry it on top of your car, in the back of a station wagon or toss it into a pick-up truck.

All of this embraces the types which make up the largest class of boats—what most persons call a rowboat, for indeed it should be rowable—which is one of its practical advantages. These boats come in all materials, but low-upkeep fiberglass is gaining the lion's share of the market among new boats. There are however, lots and lots of wooden utilities around—when properly cared for, they wear their age well.

Choose a boat with enough beam to be stable, remembering that too much beam will prevent rowing. The flatter the bottom aft, the faster the boat will be when it gets up on plane. While light construction means easy toting, if the material is too light, the boat may be too frail. Sturdiness can pay off in durability and safety. If the boat will get some rough treatment (and most fishing boats do), the bottom should be protected with longitudinal strakes. For added safety, look for some form of flotation—in air chambers or foam under the seats.

Although you can start in without a motor, you should eventually have one. Even a small one will easily triple your fishing range. Three horsepower is the safe limit. You can't make a speedboat out of a small, full-bodied craft. But even when a motor is used, see that the boat's rowlocks are located properly and have a good pair of light oars. In this service, it's sensible to have the boat handle well with oars.

BOATS FOR WATERS ONLY PARTIALLY PROTECTED

Waters that are only partially sheltered comprise the bulk of fishing waters and are used by most fishermen. Understandably, they include a great variety of water conditions, and a wide assortment of boats can be used.

Generally, 14 to 16-foot boats are best for this service, and 17 or 18-

This 14-foot aluminum utility is rated for a load of 865 pounds and a 40-h.p. motor.

footers only if conditions are unusual. In any case, you want an adequate boat, one that's oversize for its load and fast enough to get you quickly to wherever the fish are biting, and bring you back safely. Summer squalls are unpredictable, and even these partially protected waters can often get rough. Buy within this size scale, keeping in mind the number of persons you expect to carry, the distances you're likely to run, and the possible roughness of the waters. If you're trying to decide between two sizes, favor the larger. The situation is the exact opposite of that applying to sheltered waters, where a smaller boat is better than a big one. Especially for waters that are likely to get very rough, size not only means safety and comfort, but seaworthiness and speed.

Don't be overly concerned about the type of construction. All the various boat-building materials, if properly used, yield good boats. And to get a quality craft, you have only to buy a known brand. Price is another good criterion of a boat's worth, as is the reputation of the dealer handling the line. However, don't spend money on such features as highly varnished trim, lush upholstery, and fancy hardware. Instead, select a rugged, plainly fin-

A 16-foot utility can handle fairly open water and even a 9-h.p. motor will move it along at about 18 m.p.h.

ished type. Fishing boats are used much harder than are ordinary outboards. Anglers walk about in their boats more, anchor more frequently, and are likely to put in at rough docks for bait and ice.

Visualize handling or managing the boat. The seating layout should enable you to move about freely in the boat, but the less you have to move in steering and operating the motor, using the anchor, and reaching tackle and gear, the better.

Some fishing boats come exceptionally well arranged in this respect. In one corner aft there may be a live well, in the other a utility box. Another sizable storage compartment may be in the bow. Fishing chairs, or bucket seats, may be located to leave the rest of the boat uncluttered. But, from the boat manufacturer's standpoint, the difficulty is in satisfying fishermen. All fishermen have their peculiar likes and dislikes about seating arrangements, bait wells, compartments, and so on. At least one manufacturer copes with this by having approximately five different interior layouts for his 16 and 18-foot utility fisherman models.

So far as motor size is concerned, keep within recommendations for the boat, but buy in the upper limit, preferably using some form of dual motors. For example, two 15-h.p. motors are better than one 25 or 35-h.p. motor. In addition to the safety factor involved in the case of a breakdown, you'll have a better trolling outfit. An alternate motor set-up is to buy one big motor, but carry a small motor as well for trolling. A 3 to 5-h.p. will suffice. Not only will it run satisfactorily for prolonged periods at trolling speed, but it will save money on fuel and keep the big motor in better running condition. And, as with twin motors, you will not be dependent on a single engine to get back home. But, however you do it, make sure the boat you buy has a transom that will lend itself to this two-motor idea. Select a boat with a transom wide enough so that a small trolling motor can be carried more or less permanently in addition to the main motor mounted centrally.

In making your choice, consider the load—passengers and equipment— you expect to carry. Most manufacturers now attach a label to the hull indi-

This aluminum runabout is 17 feet long, has a beam of 82 inches and can handle up to the largest outboard.

cating maximum safe horsepower and maximum load. Stay well within these limits. If you are going to use the boat for fishing, you will want to be able to move around an uncluttered cockpit which should have a non-skid surface on the cockpit sole and deck. If it will be used for skiing, you will need a speed of about 25 m.p.h. and a seating arrangement which will permit an observer to fact aft (it's required in most states) and space for carrying skis, fishing rods, etc.

Some larger models provide or can be equipped with a canvas top which offers welcome relief from a burning sun as well as from a pelting cold rain.

The size of the boat will largely determine how far you can go in improving it by adding various fishing hardware or fittings. Check what experienced fishermen with similar boats have installed. Do your buying gradually, after getting to know just what will or will not make the boat more convenient for your use.

6 Cruisers

WEBSTER'S DEFINITION of a cruiser is a "powerboat equipped with cabin, permanent berths, fixed plumbing and cooking arrangements etc. necessary for living aboard."

From your standpoint, this means a boat on which you can be self-sustaining. You'll be on your own and not dependent on waterside facilities. You can stay out longer and cruise farther, an important factor when fishing is good. On lengthy cruises, you can choose the most attractive course rather than a less desirable route that's selected because it's convenient for frequent stops. Then, in rainy weather or when shore facilities and campsites are unattractive, already occupied, or perhaps not even available, you can cook, eat, and sleep aboard.

When you add live-aboard features, you increase your investment—and the dividends.

Built for maximum service in minimum size, this 19-foot stern drive has shelter, bunks forward, outriggers and a radio.

Bear in mind that these niceties call for a larger boat. As you add size, you multiply costs because of increased materials and labor to produce the boat, and the bigger powerplant you'll need to propel the boat.

The more cash you plan to invest in a boat the more critical you should be. You should also be willing to spend a bit extra to insure getting a superior boat. Look at it this way. A small outboard has a relatively easy life; it's likely to be out of the water more than it is in. But with a cruiser, the reverse might be true. The trend is to keep sizable boats stored at marinas, often in the water, rather than trailering them back and forth. This seasonal exposure to the elements is the real test of any boat's ability to withstand harsh service.

As far as convenience and comfort are concerned, you should be willing to compromise. Operating costs can be kept down by powering a boat conservatively and using its engine intelligently.

More manufacturers are producing more and better small cruisers than ever before. The incentive is the large market composed of coastal boatmen, many people who use their craft on large inland bodies of water, and those who use their boats on small waters but who are buying large outboard and inboard-outboard boats for the extra comfort and safety they offer.

Improved boat trailers have done their part, but the all-important fact is that today's large outboard and stern-drive craft are vastly superior to the pocketsized cruisers available just a few years ago. Their improved design makes them safer, faster, and better performers in bad weather and rough water. And these are the qualities important to sportsmen.

41

This 23-footer is designed for weekend cruising and fishing. Note transom fish wells.

One common feature of these boats is that they usually are beamy and have a full, high bow and good flare forward. Look for less wind-catching construction above deck, and more boat in the water. There should be a husky windshield. The bottom will have more deadrise or V than usual, giving the boat a better hold in the water and permitting a sharp wave-cutting forefoot. In sportsman models, the cockpit and interior will be designed for convenience in fishing rather than for seating for a maximum number of passengers. Even the controls will be positioned to permit handling the boat in a way most helpful to the anglers fishing astern. All these features, obviously, will not make you entirely independent of the wind and weather. Throughout the season, though, such a boat will make a tremendous difference in when and where you can go.

While single-hull boats predominate, multihull types are becoming prominent.

Don't go overboard concerning headroom. Full headroom makes for comfort, of course, but if by providing it, the cabin's height is badly out of proportion to the size of the hull, the boat will not look well. Also, its stability and seaworthiness may be questionable. Full headroom is not necessarily needed over side berths or settees; sitting headroom is enough.

(Of course, if you are particularly comfort-conscious, you can go all-out by choosing a houseboat.)

With a low shelter cabin, or cuddy, you can still have a marine head and the privacy to use it. And you can still have space for a compact galley with a two-burner stove, a small sink, and an icebox.

It is common for such a boat to have a couple of narrow berths up forward. For extra accommodations, you can sleep comfortably in the cockpit if it has a Navy top or camper top. Those folding lounge seats can provide narrow bunk space; otherwise in a large uncluttered cockpit, you can use air mattresses and summer-weight sleeping bags.

That forward cabin, incidentally, should have a hatch large enough to allow you to get through to the deck for handling anchor and dock lines. There will be times when you'll want it open for ventilation, and of course times you'll want it closed—*watertight* closed.

Because a cruiser is going to be in the water more, and subject to more rain, spray, and sun, with probably less protection, everything about it should be rugged and weather resistant. There should be no perishable materials or gingerbread frills.

Fabrics should be vinyl or synthetic-coated—resistant to mildew and rot. Any materials used on the cockpit sole or on deck should be weatherproof and non-skid.

For safety, the deck should be clear of any foot-stubbing projections. A bow rail adds a salty look, but make certain it is more than a decoration— only a sturdy rail can truly be a life-saver.

The windshield should be of safety glass and should be provided with a wiper. While a good grade of clear plastic in a strong frame will last quite satisfactorily, the abrasion from a wiper blade will destroy its transparency. Avoid plate glass; the less shatterable glass around a boat, the better.

While the design of a folding top is important, so is the quality of material, framework, and fittings. The better cover materials are marked "preshrunk." If material hasn't been so pretreated, or if it is synthetic fabric that will shrink and stretch according to the weather, the top will not be satisfac-

Cluttered cockpit is avoided by building lockers under seats for gear and tackle.

tory. Look also for double-stitching and other indications of good fabrication. Vinyl-coated frame tubing is another good sign. It's equally important that its bolts and fastenings be rustproof. Most important, make sure you can sit erect and have good vision with the top up.

From this point, it is possible to shelter the entire cockpit with the addition of top, back, and side curtains.

The extent of an overhead shelter will depend not so much on the size of the boat as on where you use it. You're adding what's called top-hamper. The weight involved is high, and there'll be enough area to catch the wind. This will affect the boat's stability and, under certain conditions, may make a small boat unsafe.

While an ice chest is bulky, and ice is heavy, the combination continues to be the best way of providing refrigeration on small cruisers. Moreover, with ice-dispensing machines becoming more numerous, there is little problem of finding ice in small quantities. Ice lasts longer in block form rather than cubed or chipped and will last even longer if kept covered with aluminum foil. A little dry ice can be used to preserve the chunk of ordinary ice, but too much of it is apt to freeze the food in the chest. Combination-type chests which take ice but also refrigerate mechanically are now available in units designed for small boats. Some operate on dockside current, or possibly on a 6 or 12-volt battery kept charged by the engine's generator or alternator.

Compact and lightweight one and two-burner stoves come in a wide variety. Used aboard boats, however, they must burn a safe fuel.

As far as utensils, dishes, and cutlery are concerned, it's not wise to do any costly buying until you know this field better. By visiting other boats, you'll find out what's suitable and what isn't. For example, some utensils are designed to nest for compact stowing; others may be intended to serve dual purposes, or shapes may be square rather than round to utilize better a stove's cooking top. If they're to be used for salt-water service, particularly where things are left aboard, stainless-steel ware is undoubtedly best. Aluminum may not actually corrode, but it takes on an uncared-for look in such service.

For ordinary boat use, favor utensils and dishes designed to meet the needs of canoeists and campers rather than items designed to appeal to car and trailer campers. Naturally, if only because of its lightness, aluminum is widely used. The plastics are displacing aluminum for dishes. Paper plates and cups are also handy to have aboard.

Some manufacturers supply their dealers with more or less bare boats, which the dealer fits out to suit the individual customer's requirements with equipment and accessories. Other manufacturers have models that can be converted by the owner for fishing or family cruising as needed.

There are a number of things you can do yourself, gradually, to convert a bare boat to your special cruising needs.

Seats can often be rearranged for more convenience. Lockers and draw-

Space-saving features here are folding louver doors and collapsible pilot seat.

ers for tackle and gear can be built beneath the seats, and bins can be built for bulkier gear. A bait well installed under a seat will be out of the way and easily within reach. Generally, whatever can be done to avoid cluttering a boat with loose gear can be considered good practice.

Your most valued convenience, the marine head, may give you cause for grief. There is a trend to prohibit overboard discharge on confined waters. That there is a growing need for restrictive antipollution measures cannot be denied and you'd best check your local situation. A number of devices are now in use on a somewhat experimental basis—chlorinators, pulverizers, incinerators. It looks like retention tanks—to be dumped overboard when offshore, or pumped out at shore stations—have the inside track as the ultimate solution.

To live aboard—even for a weekend—will mean a need for warm and dry spare clothes, personal toilet articles and at least a minimum of bed linens and blankets. All of these are going to consume space, and necessarily the best, driest, most protected space. Some boats provide lockers under berths for folded clothes and bed linens, and a small hanging locker where you can hang a dress and jacket for shoreside attire.

Regardless of size, boats must also have certain equipment aboard, such as government-required life preservers and a fire extinguisher. Other must items include the usual tools and spare parts, a distress signal kit, an anchor, a length of anchorline, and a bailing device of some kind.

However it's done, with spare containers or with built-in tanks, an adequate supply of fuel must be carried. If spare containers are used, they should be secured against shifting. Batteries should similarly be chocked or held down.

One important consideration to keep in mind as you add live-aboard gear on a small boat: the boat's trim, the level at which the hull rides, is critical to the boat's general behavior. Play it safe—don't overload.

45

7   Pontoon Boats and Houseboats

ONE OF the nicer things that has happened on the waterfront since the days of Huck Finn is that rafts and shanty boats have become respectable. In place of Huck's raft, he'd find a pontoon-supported platform with gaily striped awning; instead of a dank shanty boat stuck in the mud, there would be an air-conditioned houseboat ready to cast off and zoom down the river at 40 m.p.h.

Huck would surely be smart enough to ignore the frills and quickly size up the advantages gained in the transition. Nor should any sportsman fail to appraise the true values of these modern pontoon boats and houseboats.

A number of fishermen have made admirable use of those raft-like floats made up of a pair of long, cigar-shaped steel or aluminum cylinders or pontoons, a connecting framework, and a plywood deck. Sometimes these floats are anchored well offshore where they serve as roomy and stable fishing platforms. Just as many fishermen, though, use a small motor mounted astern of a float to troll in the conventional way.

A survey conducted at the time of the New York Boat Show in January of 1966 indicated there were forty-five manufacturers of houseboats and pontoon boats who attempted to distribute their products beyond a purely local

Anglers often prefer open models like this one. Motor's mount is adjustable.

Pontoon supported deck makes a stable fishing platform. It can carry 1,480 pounds and handle up to 35 h.p. motor.

market. One of the factors which limit widespread distribution of their boats is the cost and difficulty of shipping. Those with more than 8-foot beams require special permits for highway shipment.

Prices of these stock boats ranged from about $500 for something resembling a 10-foot floating porch, to about $23,000 for a 52-foot, three-bedroom floating home. Of course for customized versions, you can spend as much as you care to part with. While some hulls are of fiberglass or fiberglass over wood, the majority by far are built of steel or aluminum.

The smaller craft are propelled by a single or twin outboard installation; stern drives are proving popular on the larger models.

You'll find single-hull construction and catamarans. The former are apt to be faster, the latter more stable. One manufacturer claims speeds in excess of 30 m.p.h. for his 30-footer with single 210 h.p. engine, and speeds of 40 m.p.h. for his 40-footer with twin 210's.

Pontoon craft have a surprisingly large load capacity. A 16-footer will take as much as a 1,000-pound load and a 20-footer twice that. So far as power is concerned, 5 to 18-h.p. motors usually are recommended for the 16-footers, while the 20-footers may take up to 40 h.p. The boats maneuver quite well considering their hull shape, and those driven by the larger motors move fast.

The next step up from these simple craft is to what's best called the pontoon day cruiser. Characteristic features are a demountable or permanent canvas canopy and a deck railing. Most manufacturers of these cruisers offer a host of features, some as standard equipment and others as optional extras. All are designed for comfortable living aboard and for convenience of operation. Usually some provision is made for lowering or removing the shelter so the boat can go under low bridges when afloat and on the highway when

Big pontoon boat has a large load capacity, yet can operate in shoal water.

Light draft, husky pontoons make this type suitable for shoal-stream fishing.

trailering. Front and rear sections of the deck railing may be filled in solid, and canvas curtains for buttoning down against rain are often available. Steering and motor controls that lead to a captain's steering console or stand with a steering wheel are common. There may even be a helmsman's swivel chair. The motor mount, usually a standard feature, may be adjustable to permit operation in very shallow water. Though movable deck chairs are often used, there may be several built-in seats with padded backs. An ice chest may also be a built-in feature. Some models even have a built-in combination bar and compact galley.

Possibly the ultimate feature in this day-cruiser type is a more-or-less permanent cabin structure. Built-in features, such as a galley, berths for two or four persons, a dining table, and lockers are usually housed in a waist-high solid structure. This is topped by a pipe framework supporting a canvas top with windows in the sides and ends. This craft is basically a houseboat, but it has wider decks for fishing and lounging and no effort is made to provide maximum cabin accommodations. Compared with the conventional houseboat, this type is lightweight, possibly 1,500 pounds in aluminum, and can be driven by a relatively small motor. The pontoon cruiser has another advantage over the houseboat in that its canvas top can be lowered. When it is, wind resistance is appreciably reduced, a desirable feature if the cruiser is kept at a mooring for lengthy periods and also when it is being trailered.

With twin 210-h.p. marine engines, this 40-footer belies her portliness with speeds of 40 m.p.h.

Most manufacturers offer a choice of steel or aluminum models, and the latter appear to be selling exceptionally well, particularly in the larger sizes. Each builder stresses the structural advantages of his own boats, of course, but modern pontoon craft are generally well designed and built. For both steel and aluminum models, steps are taken to insure easy maintenance and long life. If the boat is used in normal service, some manufacturers are able to make extensive guarantees—up to ten years in some cases—against punctured or ruptured pontoons. These builders use aluminum specially suited to marine applications, well-finished parts, rugged deck girders closely spaced atop husky pontoon attachments, and bracing or reinforcing at points of greatest strain or wear. In any case, the manufacturer undoubtedly will have provided against a pontoon failing entirely in the event of a puncture. The common method is to weld in bulkheads to form several sealed compartments within the pontoon. Another method is to fill the pontoon with waterproof flotation material.

These day-cruiser models, usually 20 to 28 feet long, have many uses. Some fishermen prefer the canopied type, others go for the open, less completely equipped boats. You can start with an open boat and progressively improve it by making your own pipe and canvas top and gradually adding features.

Pontoon day cruisers are fine for day-long family outings with stops made to anchor or to run the boat ashore for lunch or to fish or swim. Though they are classed as day cruisers, these boats really pay their way in pleasure when used for weekend or vacation-time boat-camping trips.

Pontoon craft are not intended for use on rough water, but they are ideal for small rivers, streams, chains of small lakes connected by creeks, marshy expanses, and all sheltered waterways. Because of their very shallow draft and sturdiness, even large pontoon boats can be taken up waterways that are too shallow and rock-strewn for a conventional boat of comparable size. You can carry a lot of camping gear on pontoon craft. Instead of anchoring, you can run right up onto a shelving shore and get off over the bow. If the shore is unsuitable for a camp, you can stay aboard quite comfortably.

Pontoon boat's shape is well suited to trailering. Weight is centered low.

A large houseboat like this 65-footer makes a luxurious base of operations on a resort lake.

These boats lend themselves well to trailering provided the trailer is designed and fitted out to take the hull configuration. The boat's shape is squat and the weight is centered low. The shallow draft simplifies launching and reloading. Most manufacturers can supply matching trailers. The cost of a heavy-duty model is around $450.

You might be surprised what a houseboat can do for you.

They are made to order for the skipper who is frustrated by any reluctance on the part of his wife. Landlubber complaints usually have the somewhat justifiable basis of cramped quarters and lack of headroom. A houseboat can mean stand-up rather than stoop-and-squat space; full-size beds rather than cramped bunks; complete kitchen rather than a make-do galley. Even the stability of a houseboat and the fact that it is customarily used on protected waters can add to that "just like home" security. In short, it offers a mobile weekend cottage without traffic jams.

The names some of the manufacturers use should be enough to lure just about anyone with that urge to get away—Lazy Days, Drift-R-Cruz, River Queen, Holiday, Sylvan; and how about Flotel and Boatel for the timorous.

Outfitters and camp operators are using modern houseboats to accommodate fishermen in the summer and hunting parties in the fall. In the latter case, the boat is moved, usually by a pair of outboards, to some outlying spot, where the party ranges out from it for the day's hunt, using canoes or skiffs. Similarly, numerous individual owners of houseboats are finding their craft a good substitute for the old-time hunting or fishing camp. You can move the boat wherever you think the best sport will be had.

8 Collapsible Craft

(INFLATABLE & FOLDING)

THE TREND toward ownership of larger outboards and the growing popularity of inboard-outboards are promoting considerable interest among outdoorsmen in small, portable craft—rubber boats, folding boats or kayaks, and collapsible canvas rigs. It makes good sense to them to have one of these as a second boat to use on confined waters and on waters where horsepower restrictions apply or motors are banned. These craft also appeal to campers because they can be carried without a trailer.

Some fishermen want an ultralight boat they can backpack to remote ponds and potholes, and some duck hunters want such a boat largely for retrieving on isolated waters to which they must hike with a boat on the back. There are also those who want a light boat that can be carried by a horse or in a small plane, and some want boats they can keep in an apartment.

All of these share one common interest so far as boat ownership is concerned. That is portability. They want boats that can be easily carried and stored, and the choice of craft offering these features is now wide and varied.

Many owners of large outboards and stern-drive boats are now following the inboard cruiser's practice of using a small boat as a tender. While the inboard's owner usually prefers a rigid dinghy or small boat, the outboarder is better off with an inflatable or demountable type. The inboard is often big enough so that the dinghy can be carried in davits astern or overturned on the cabin top. Aboard the average big outboard or stern-drive, however, the tender should be deflatable or demountable so that it occupies a minimum of space. There'll be times when the outboarder will tow the small craft astern, such as when cruising a winding waterway with frequent stops to sample the fishing. Otherwise, towing a tender cuts your speed and can be dangerous on open or rough waters.

A tender pays off when you use your larger boat for cruising, exploring, and overnight camping. You will often want to use the small boat for side trips. If there's wooded shoreline, you'll be able to fish it more effectively with the smaller boat. The tender's also useful for streams too shallow or snag-infested for your big boat. If there are children along, they'll have fun in the tender and get some savvy about boats. Carrying a second boat also gives you confidence on open waters. It's survival equipment in a fire or other emergency.

THE INFLATABLE BOATS

The rubber raft's popularity for fishing and hunting started with the rafts sold as government surplus following World War II. Their condition ranged from new to badly worn, but offerings were plentiful and prices low. In the main, these rafts served the average buyer quite well. Much of the same can be said for today's surplus rafts except that offerings are scarcer. There are few, if any, regular sources of supply. In buying, one should deal only with known and reliable concerns, since the only guide to a raft's condition is the seller's say-so.

Sizes range from one-man rafts without oarlocks or seat to huge, round twenty-man rafts. The in-between sizes are popular for running swift rivers. A five-man raft, 9 feet long, actually has enough buoyancy to support twice that number of persons, which creates a tendency to overrate the carrying capacity. However, lack of leg room and elbow room is probably a deterrant to overloading by sportsmen not intent upon mere survival. Prices depend largely upon supply and demand for the particular sizes. A raft of medium size is likely to have two inflation chambers as a safety feature. If it is heavy, and the rubberized fabric is still in good condition, such a raft should withstand a remarkable amount of harsh usage.

You will find those one and two-man designations somewhat deceptive. For solo use, except for retrieving purposes and short periods of fishing, select the two-man size. Otherwise, with two adults, you're crowded. A four-man size is better if two are fishing. Length and breadth figures can also fool you. Those air chambers, 10 or 12 inches in diameter, cut down your usable space.

Angler packs deflated raft on his back to remote pond.

Minutes after arrival, he's fishing.

In the low-priced bracket, say under $125, are the imported inflatables which have in the past sold for as low as $50. Also, there are some cheap American rafts best used only with supervision as children's play boats. Judging from worthwhile rafts made in this country, it seems impossible to produce a quality product with features intended for sportsmen for under around $250. You can buy in the low-priced field only to try out the idea of owning a raft for occasional use. If the second boat idea proves satisfactory, you can then invest in a better craft.

You can get boat-shaped models that avoid the conventional blunt-ended raft shape. It's difficult to row a blunt-ended raft if the wind is blowing, and they perform poorly with motors. Boat or dory-shaped models handle nearly as well as a skiff of the same size would and the square stern is designed to take a small motor and utilize its power reasonably well. These rafts or boats are better made since they are intended for continuous service rather than emergency use.

Materials now used by the larger manufacturers, mainly Dacron or nylon impregnated with neoprene, or du Pont's Hypalon-based rubber, simplify maintenance and lengthen the craft's life. These fabrics and coatings are highly impervious to oil, rot, and even the effects of strong sunlight. One no longer has to avoid exposing his inflatable unduly to the weather or be overly careful in drying it off before packing. Special paints can be had, but they are used mostly to change the color scheme. Intelligently used and decently cared for, a modern inflatable should give from five to ten years of service.

There'll be three or more separate air cells as a safety feature. Inflation and deflation are simpler, and the valves and other gear are designed to last as long as the raft itself.

In some makes, the forward section has been drawn out to give a bluntly sharp and possibly raised bow. Some models could be called canoe-shaped. There are also the new, so-called banana models, similarly double-ended but with higher and blunter ends. Still others, notably the runabouts and some sailing models, are twin-hulled. One manufacturer even offers a pair of the inflatable floats along with instructions for completing the boat. There are also those offerings which, while not true inflatables, are similar enough to be highly popular with sportsmen. One is a folding kayak that has integral air chambers. Another, a very durable, rigid boat resembling the conventional raft, has a high safety rating.

Shape is an important factor. The shapelier the craft the easier it will be to paddle or to row. The beamier it is the more stable, but the greater the need for using a motor. In any case, don't expect an inflatable to handle like a conventional boat. An inflatable can be hard to control in a strong wind. If the water is rough, paddling or rowing to windward will be hard work. But you'll be safe. Inflatables are so buoyant that waves merely lift them. If some water splashes aboard, you just bail it out. For such reasons, an inflatable, properly handled, makes a fair boat for use in the surf.

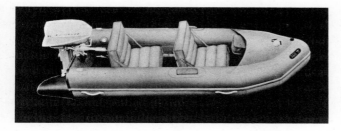

Inflatable runabout maneuvers almost as well as rigid craft.

Excepting the double-enders, most makes are now designed to take a motor. A few have a plywood transom. On others, a mount made to suit the particular model is fitted or can be had as an extra. Motors up to five h.p. are usually recommended. That's enough, since these craft drive easily up to five or six miles an hour and can't safely be pushed faster.

Inflating and deflating these craft have been made easier. Check what the manufacturer says about the valves. These used to give a lot of trouble, but now a reputable line of inflatables is likely to have valves that are well

Avon 9-foot Redcrest inflatable has a 1,090-pound bouyancy, takes 3-h.p. motor.

made, not likely to corrode, be well secured, and operate satisfactorily. Pumping is ordinarily done by a hand pump or a foot bellows supplied as standard equipment. Inflating may take as little as five minutes, deflating half that. Electric-operated, low-pressure pumps can be had but aren't necessary. Some manufacturers will provide CO_2 inflation at extra cost, perhaps $35 for a two-man boat. Most makes of these boats are designed for inflating with a pump limited to a certain pressure, say 2 pounds per square inch. But the air chambers are designed to withstand a much higher pressure.

Check to see what's standard equipment. Rowlocks should be well-made and strongly secured. Some rafts sold for live-saving purposes don't have them. There should be provision for hanging onto the boat and for helping to right it in the event of a capsize. Lines are usually fitted, but see to it that their keepers are well-secured. The same goes for a bow-mooring ring. In some models, the seats are of plywood, in others they are simply wide strips of heavy rubber or they may be of the inflatable type. Some even have matching

Nautisport Speedyak, deflated, fits into a 20″ x 30″ x 8″ bag.

backrests. Some boats have floor racks that may be slatted and rolled up compactly. Still others have the bottom beefed up. In one make, an air mattress does double duty as a floor. Paddles are usually the double-bladed spoon type, jointed for carrying or use as singles. Oars may be wood or aluminum, the latter having sealed air chambers so they'll float. These are more or less the essentials, and understandably the extent and quality of such features are likely to be in keeping with the price of the craft.

Extras should also be considered. As often as not, there'll be a lengthy list. Most extras, especially if foreign-made, are attractively priced.

The marketing setup for inflatables is unusual. Unless your local dealer is exceptional, you won't be impressed by his stock, if any, of inflatables. Buying direct either from the manufacturer, mail order house, or a distributor is still the rule.

One thing you'll notice about inflatables is that each manufacturer has his own ideas on models or shapes. The trend is definitely away from the life raft form, though this shape provides maximum floatation and stability.

A typical boat-shaped, three-man, 10-footer will have around 44 inches of beam and will weigh about 80 pounds. Deflated, it packs in a 39-inch-long, 15-inch-diameter case with handles for carrying. An inflatable craft of this sort is usually priced at up to $250.

Among the better imports are inflatable outboard runabouts. They have the bulky look characteristic of inflatable craft, but they are fast and perform well in shallow water, including turbulent rivers and ocean surf. Some are priced at up to $500. Specifications for a typical 10-footer are: 5-foot beam, transom to take motors up to 25 h.p., speeds of around 30 miles an hour, neoprene-coated nylon fabric, and four air chambers.

Smaller imported rubber boats of matching quality, but designed for rowing or use with a smaller motor, are priced around $125 for a 7-foot two-seater. Another model popular with sportsmen is kayak-shaped. An 11-footer with seats for two paddlers and provision for mounting a very small motor on the side weighs around 30 pounds. Prices are in the $150 range. Repair kits are available along with such optional extras as a high-volume foot pump, motor bracket, sectional oars or double paddles, etc. Sometimes these items are included in the purchase price as standard equipment.

THE FOLDING BOATS

Quality inflatables produced in this country have not been good sellers, possibly because of the rather high pricing in comparison with surplus rubber rafts. The opposite applies for folding craft, including kayaks, and collapsible canvas boats and canoes. Both general types have always been popular with sportsmen, particularly as second boats. The quality of offerings generally has been high, and these craft are usually remarkably long-lived. There is a wide choice of models and sizes. Most manufacturers sell directly to customers. Despite keen foreign competition, American manufacturers have been able to compete favorably on pricing, workmanship, and quality of materials.

The folding, laminated-wood framework of folding kayaks and quality-grade folding runabouts is ingeniously engineered. Such framing couples lightness and strength. When the framework is locked in place and the covering is secured, the boat has the feel of a rigid craft. Ordinarily, assembly is a 15-minute job, but it can be done in less time as one becomes familiar with the boat. The hull portion of the covering usually is made of a special multiply fabric, heavily impregnated and surfaced on both sides with vinyl. Despite a thickness of 3/32-in., this skin is quite flexible. Though the covering is strong and its resiliency helps to soften impacts with rocks or snags, the hull can be punctured by a sharply pointed object. Such accidental damage can be quickly repaired with adhesive tape. Permanent repairs are made with plastic cement. The deck is lighter in weight but it is also vinyl-coated. For hull and deck, there's a choice of color combinations and the color is impregnated to simplify maintenance.

Basic sizes in folding kayaks are 15 feet and 17½ feet. The smaller one is considered a single-seater, the larger accommodates two paddlers and even a third person. Both sizes are designed for easy paddling but they will take a very small outboard motor on a special side bracket available as an extra. For carrying and to simplify shipping, the parts pack in two bags: one 26 x 24 x 5 inches, containing the folded hull and all crossframes, and another 54 x 10 x 8 inches to take the longitudinal parts and the jointed double paddles. Total weight (around 55 pounds for the 15-foot boat; 75 pounds for the larger model) is thus about evenly divided.

The runabout model weighs around 125 pounds for a 14-footer. Its rigid stern takes up to 7½ h.p. motors, giving cruising speeds up to 15 m.p.h.

In addition to these basic kayak models, there are others for speed paddling, heavy-duty service, and so on. There's an imposing array of equipment available, including ultralightweight tents and compact camping gear for those interested in kayak cruising.

Collapsible canvas boats and canoes are produced in the U.S., have an established reputation for durability, and are realistically priced. The choice includes 12, 14, and 16-foot canoes; 9 to 14-foot, double-ended boats intended for rowing, and 10 to 16-foot, square-stern models, for use with outboard motors. There's a wide choice of extra equipment.

Assembled Kayak looks like a conventional model; motor mounts on side.

In carrying bags, kayak fits confined space of car trunk.

Everything about these collapsible craft is functional. The color, unless specially ordered, is a serviceable brown. The steel framework consists of longitudinal members which fit into reinforced pockets sewn in the canvas covering, plus ribs which go into metal holders in the gunwales. All are then locked in place with a wooden keel, and floorboards distribute weight over the bottom. The hull covering, which is stretched taut during assembly, is made of heavy, 22-ounce canvas specially treated and guaranteed to stand up under hard usage. Collapsed for carrying, the craft packs in a single bag (two bags for the larger boats with square sterns). The collapsed boat is roughly one third the length of the assembled boat. Weights range from 65 to 85 pounds for canoes; 50 to 95 for the double-ended boats, and 60 to 130 for those with square sterns.

In addition to the two standard types—inflatables and folding craft—there are others which are offered from time to time. Skiffs with plywood sides and bottoms and watertight hinges that fold flat for carrying have been offered occasionally. Sectional boats are made in two or three separate units designed to nest inside each other for carrying. Then there are tube floats which accommodate a single person. Among the latest offerings is a float consisting of a circular fiberglass unit floating in a heavy tractor inner tube. Power can be either an electric trolling motor or a hand-operated flipper motor. The outfit weighs around 50 pounds and needs 18 inches of water to float in. In other floats, you sit in a seat attached to a canvas holder which encases the inner tube. Your legs go through holes in the seat so that you can walk on the bottom in shallow water. If it's cold you can wear waders. Paddle pushers, attached to your feet, provide propulsion in deeper water. These are an optional extra. Total cost is around $35, but the buyer supplies his own inner tube.

9   Boats for Hunting

WHEN FALL comes, and your boating buddies ring down the curtain on their season, resist the trend; be a holdout. This is the best time of the year. Your favorite waters will be less crowded, your favorite stopping places will be insect-free and the scenery more colorful. And then there is hunting! Your boat can make you the most successful hunter in town.

Contrary to what many persons think, boats used for hunting today need not be of the traditional hunting design or construction. Conventional outboard boats, skiffs, johnboats, auto-tops, canoes, and kayaks now predominate in hunting service. While it is true that the average boat can usually be improved for its owner's particular brand of hunting, the main point is that it can be used and, in many cases, that it may mean the difference between its owner being able to hunt or not.

AS TRANSPORTATION AND AS SHOOTING PLATFORM

Boats can be utilized to get to areas that can't be reached in any other way. This effectively eliminates competition from hunters who either must walk or use cars. Boat owners also have an edge on fellow hunters when it comes to locating such areas. They can scout likely hunting territory during the summer while fishing or cruising. They can explore areas adjacent to small lakes, rivers, swamps, marshes, and backwoods potholes which, because they are accessible only by boat, may be veritable game pockets. Cutover land often offers fine hunting possibilities. Some of the best grouse shooting might be along old logging trails so overgrown they can't be negotiated by any vehicle. Perhaps a creek will give access into the area.

Float boating along streams and rivers is an excellent means of locating potential hunting hotspots. Such waterways often course through areas too difficult to reach by hunters who don't have boats. These isolated spots often provide a wealth of small-game hunting, varmint shooting, and waterfowling.

The almost limitless opportunities provided by float boating not only for fishing and camping but also for hunting, are largely responsible for the current revival of interest in canoes. A few years ago, only a few manufacturers produced canoes. Today over three dozen companies are offering them in a wide range of models, sizes, and prices.

Small, aluminum boat in dead-grass color can serve dual purposes—hunting, fishing.

Houseboats are becoming commonplace in the hunting picture. The decked pontoon types are often stripped of their canvas shelters, camouflaged, and used as floating duck blinds. Some owners of houseboats with permanently mounted cabins will move their boats after Labor Day to isolated river locations, anchoring or tying them to the shore to serve as fall hunting lodges. A small boat is then used to get back and forth, and for side trips taken from the moored mother craft.

Small cruisers are being used more extensively to provide living accommodations on weekend hunting trips. Large, high-powered, open runabouts are also used by hunters as a means of getting into country that can be reached only by water.

So far as waterfowling is concerned, nearly all types of craft can be used. Large, open outboards serve well for traveling open waters, often with a small boat towed astern for use on the shooting grounds. In many cases, these big and fast craft permit traveling to areas that would be impossible to reach in smaller boats. And, with only a given number of hours available, such a boat enables one to devote more time to the actual hunt.

Small, highly specialized hunting craft are usually used only on the body of water for which they were originally developed. Examples are: the sneak floats, scull boats and gunning dories of the Northeastern coastal states, Delaware River duckers and tuckups, the Susquehanna bushwack rig, Mississippi scull boats, Reelfoot boats, St. Clair drift boats, the Dan Kidney hunting boats, and the Barnegat Bay sneak box. With the exception of the Barnegat Bay sneak box, which is now produced in molded fiberglass by a New Jersey builder, these boats are difficult or impossible to obtain unless you live in the area where they're built and deal directly with small, local builders. More widely distributed hunting boats are sensibly designed to suit a variety of gunning conditions.

The local, specialized types are intended for waterfowl hunting and are seldom used for other purposes. The usefulness of such a boat nowadays is limited. Generally, it is unwise to transplant these boats. They have been developed over the years to suit local conditions, and other waters may call for an entirely different boat. For waterfowling, however, it is sensible to investigate any specialized type popular on the marsh or body of water you expect to hunt. It's likely to be a real shooting asset, and the cost can be offset by a lifetime of service that such a boat usually gives if it's looked after intelligently during the off season.

Personally, however, I'm all for the multi-purpose small boat. If you already have a fair-size boat and a trailer, you're equipped to negotiate larger bodies if water. The small boat, carried on or in your car, can be used to get back into small bodies of water where a larger boat's speed and size might make it a nuisance. With two boats, you're not as likely to be at the mercy of the weather. If it's too cold or windy on the larger waters, you can always seek some small, sheltered waterway in your small boat. You're also well-equipped for extended family boating and boat-camping trips.

For hunting, use your big boat to reach places that are inaccessible by car or on foot. You'll also use it to freight in your gear, and—if it's a live-aboard type—as a movable shelter. Carry the small hunting boat aboard or tow it, and use it to hunt shallow or weed-infested areas.

Inflatable craft are easily carried into remote areas that are difficult to reach and to hunt by any other means.

Broad-beamed boat is needed if it is used as a blind and hunters stand to shoot.

Each fall, deer hunters trailer husky outboard rigs long distances. They launch their boats, load their gear aboard, and set out across a lake or up a river to a campsite in a remote area. In a way, they are using canoe tactics, but unless they've brought a smaller boat along, they're not as well-equipped for hunting as the canoeist. With a large boat, the hunters are confined to deeper, comparatively obstacle-free waters. But the large boat does provide several advantages. The hunting party can get deeper into back country in a limited time and with much less effort. The larger boat will carry more gear and food, and there should be no difficulty moving the kill out of the woods in it.

In modern waterfowling, gunners use seaworthy, fast boats to reach remote shooting grounds and to freight gear and supplies to outlying camps. Some gunners carry a portable or demountable blind to camouflage the boat. Others take along materials with which to build a blind, or merely run the boat into tall grass or reeds, using the natural, local vegetation to hide it.

You should familiarize yourself with the laws that govern hunting from a boat. Local and state laws are often more restrictive than federal laws. For example, federal law permits shooting migratory birds from a boat with an outboard motor attached as long as the motor is tipped up, clearly not in use. Many states, however, require that the motor be physically removed from the boat before game can be legally shot. Whatever the law, running down on waterfowl in a fast boat is not only despicable; it is certain to drive the birds out of the area.

A small boat for shooting should be stable and easy to row or paddle, but a small motor, particularly a gearshift model, is handy for placing decoys, pursuing cripples, and picking up dead birds. Learn to maneuver the boat in reverse, and pick up the birds over the transom. Remember that very small boats are not foolproof. Learn to allow for their shortcomings.

HUNTING TECHNIQUES

At first, it's best to limit yourself to meandering streams or small rivers. Almost every area has confined waterways that provide good shooting if they're hunted intelligently. Jump shooting at ducks, picking squirrels out of trees along the bank, and varmint shooting from a small boat are good sport.

If you don't know your section intimately, start by studying a detailed map. Look for promising stretches between bridges over small streams and rivers. Most hunters seldom work streams more than a mile away from places where they can park. This often leaves you a choice of waters leading through country that seldom sees a hunter.

Twelve-foot fiberglass duckboat weighs only 160 pounds, has carrying handles, flotation.

This kind of hunting calls for a lightweight, maneuverable boat. Whether you use a motor depends on your preferences, the depth of the water, the obstacles in the stream, and the laws. The most productive stretches are usually those on which the boat must be paddled or poled.

If the water is reasonably deep and snag-free, work upstream with the motor, checking for birds or game. Then shoot while drifting back down, and use the paddle or an oar only to keep clear of the banks. Silent drifting is usually more productive than rowing, paddling, or using the motor. If practical, remove the motor and stow it inside the boat. Apart from regulations

Airboat with "airplane" rudder can travel extremely shallow water.

prohibiting hunting under power, you will find that landowners seldom object if a motor is not being used. Figure on at least two hours to float back down for every hour spent motoring upstream—more if the stretch is promising.

If you're not using a motor, launch your boat well upstream and have someone meet you with the car at a preselected bridge downstream. Figure about two miles per hour as good floating speed since you may take a ramble ashore now and then. In the fall, the borders of many small streams produce nuts, mushrooms, fruits, and berries as well as game. Make your first float on a new stream short; you may encounter unknown obstacles.

On longer floats, use a motor to travel uninteresting stretches, but float more promising water. Many streams and rivers are long enough to provide a full day's float. By carrying light camping gear and food, you can camp overnight. Quite often, you can end your trip at a town downstream, leave your rig in someone's care, and take public transportation back home. More boat liveries and fishing camps are going into the float-trip business. They cater largely to hunters and nature lovers as a way of extending the season. Most of them prefer to rent a boat and pick it up at some set point downstream.

By paddling quietly directly beneath squirrels, you can pick off some that you wouldn't have seen from shore. Often the best duck shooting occurs on bends and curves in the stream. Stay on the inside of bends when you approach. Mallards tend to gather on curves, but they are jumpy. Black ducks hide almost anywhere, and you must keep your eyes open for singles. Camouflaging the boat or canoe pays off when you're sneaking up on mallards, but it doesn't seem to make much difference with blacks.

Don't shoot while standing up in a small boat. At all times, keep your weight low. Since you'll often use a paddle or single oar, learn the Indian paddling position, kneeling on a cushion in the bottom with your rump against the edge of a seat or thwart. Particularly if it's windy, paddle amidships, not in the stern. In this position, your gun can be kept handy, you can swing from the waist when shooting, and your weight placement in the boat is right for maximum stability.

Be especially careful about shooting into trees lining the bank; it's often hard to tell what's behind them. When shooting near or on the water, remember that bullets can ricochet off the surface.

When gunning from a low duck boat or sneak box, the wise gunner lies flat, pretty much concealed, with his gun safely across his legs. From this position, you can sit up in one motion with your feet hooked under the gunwales or deck and swing from the waist. Be particularly careful when gunning with a partner from a small craft with a confined cockpit.

Always wear life jackets on deep water, and select a style that won't hinder your movements. Even on seemingly safe waters, keep seat-cushion life preservers handy. Remember that the heavy boots and bulky clothing worn during the hunting season could easily drag you to the bottom.

HOW TO RIG YOUR BOAT FOR HUNTING

In rigging your boat for hunting, keep these three points in mind: 1. Your personal safety and comfort. 2. The welfare of your boat and motor. 3. Improving your boat for hunting. Factors determining what should be done in these respects are the weather, your boat's type and size, and the manner in which you expect to use the craft.

Except in the South, you should be prepared for freezing weather during the hunting season. Your motor should be in good running condition to insure easy starting. If spark plugs haven't been replaced all season, put in a new set. If you depend on electric starting, keep the battery well charged. Check the grease in the lower unit—the case must be full. The grease should be fresh and in good condition or it will channel while operating in cold water. If the motor becomes progressively harder to start as the weather gets colder, there may be dirt or water in the fuel system, a common cold-weather problem. The remedy is a thorough cleaning of the fuel tank and the fuel screen in the carburetor. In cold weather, you must also pay more attention to the thoroughness of your mixing of fuel.

The worst effect of cold weather on a motor is the freezing of its cooling system. This can't occur when your motor is running, but it can happen very quickly when it is out of use. The preventive measure is simple—drain the motor properly after each use. Don't merely let the water run out. Take the motor off the transom, hold it upright and revolve the flywheel several times while shaking the motor from side to side. Because no precautions against freezing need be taken with small air-cooled outboard motors, they are very much in demand for hunting service.

For the boat itself, the chief hazard in fall hunting is ice. Thin ice, the kind that skims the water during a still, cold night, has much more of a cutting effect than thicker ice. Aluminum and fiberglass boats, even heavily fiberglassed wood boats, are virtually immune to damage by such ice. But the ordinary light, all-wood, or plywood boat's planking can be chewed up, even cut through, in a surprisingly short time.

There are two main methods of protecting boats from such damage. If it is a heavy skiff, sheet metal, preferably copper, tacked along the waterline and carried well up the bow will do the trick. This method involves low cost and, if desired, the metal can be removed later for ordinary use of the boat. However, with typical factorybuilt outboards or other light craft, the planking will likely be too thin to take heavy tacks or copper nails which must be used as fastenings. Fiberglass, two layers of the heavy-duty grade, will afford permanent protection without marring the boat's appearance. The fiberglass can be put on only along the waterline, or on the bottom and sides up to above the waterline. While you're at it, though, it's wise to fiberglass the hull completely. Then, in addition to being well protected, the boat should be truly leakproof. A boat that leaks is a particular nuisance in cold weather. Water collecting in the bilge will freeze and must be broken out. Too much ice in the bilge will destroy the boat's safety features, and, particularly in a chine-type hull, it can strain or damage the craft.

Emergency protection against ice, should you have to break a path back to your launching site, can be had by suspending a pair of poles or planks, fastened together to form a V, from the gunwales forward to bear against the bow in snow-plough fashion. Understandably, however your boat is protected, you should run slowly in cutting your way through thin ice. If you must break a path through thicker ice, with a hull that will stand it, run the boat, with its bow well up, at slow speed onto the ice. Then shift your weight forward, rocking the boat from side to side, if necessary. With that patch broken, back off and repeat the process.

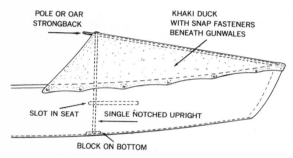

POLE OR OAR STRONGBACK

KHAKI DUCK WITH SNAP FASTENERS BENEATH GUNWALES

SLOT IN SEAT   SINGLE NOTCHED UPRIGHT

BLOCK ON BOTTOM

Hood rig helps to camouflage boat and protects occupants from wind and spray.

The accompanying sketches show methods of improving small boats for hunting service. Spray hoods range from simple stick-held affairs to tailored folding-canvas dodgers. If the boat is to serve as a blind, khaki duck rather than white canvas should be used. Try littering the bottom of your boat with straw. You can make yourself a nest to keep warm and dry, and when you leave the boat, use the straw to cover and hide tell-tale equipment that might spook the flying ducks.

Occasionally, one sees a removable forward deck. In any case, the idea is to keep flying spray out of the boat and to be protected against the wind. Staying comfortable afloat in cold weather is largely a matter of not getting wet and keeping out of the wind.

Shelters of this sort additionally provide dry storage space for guns and gear. Decoys, however they're carried, should be kept in an orderly way. Each block should have its line and anchor neatly wound around it so there'll be no tangling. Some gunners prefer ordinary bushel baskets for carrying decoys in, while others have folding or take-apart racks which fasten to their boat's forward deck. Remember that stowing each block properly, as it is taken in, will save you a lot of aggravation on the next trip.

Rather than anchoring a boat in the conventional manner in shallow water, many experienced gunners prefer to use a pair of slim poles or saplings shoved through a pair of special holders and down into the mud. Then

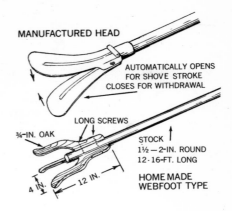

MANUFACTURED HEAD

AUTOMATICALLY OPENS
FOR SHOVE STROKE
CLOSES FOR WITHDRAWAL

LONG SCREWS

¾-IN. OAK

STOCK
1½ — 2-IN. ROUND
12-16-FT. LONG

HOME MADE
WEBFOOT TYPE

4 IN.   12 IN.

Pushpole moves boat faster than
paddle, permits safe standing to
see over reeds.

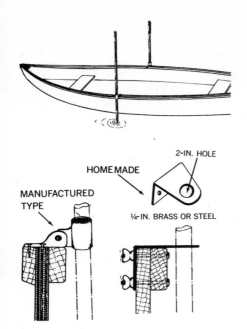

2-IN. HOLE

HOME MADE

MANUFACTURED
TYPE

¼-IN. BRASS OR STEEL

Poles, loose in holders and driven
in mud, keep boat steady in shallow water.

the boat can't swing about. This method is an adaptation of the pole-tube feature common on duck boats, but it's easier on the boat in choppy water. Most holders mount as a pair on the gunwales.

Ammunition is best carried, along with other shooting gear, in a water-proof box. Most are homemade and usually serve some dual purpose. Some boats have two such boxes, which also serve as shooting seats. The top may be padded with foam rubber, or a swivel-type rowboat seat may be attached to it. Sometimes the boat's regular seats are made removable so that the boxes can be used in their place.

For marsh travel, or where the water is uniformly shallow, take a push-pole along. You can make better time than with a paddle, and you can safely stand, using the pole to balance yourself, to look over tall grass or reeds. The end of the pole should be fitted with either a patented head or homemade feet. In any case, have an extra paddle along, a sponge, and a proper bailer. Too much water in the bottom of a small boat makes it easy to slip and dan-gerously lessens its stability.

Whether or not you camouflage your boat, and to what extent, depends on its type and the nature of your hunting. A canoe or other light craft used for float hunting needn't be specially painted or otherwise camouflaged. But where a boat is used as a floating blind, the more it is made to appear as part of the local water scene the better. If it is a hunting type, used more or less exclusively for waterfowling, it undoubtedly will be painted a dead-grass

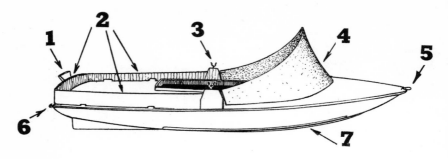

1. Motor Mount
2. Decoy Rack (Removable)
3. Oarlocks
4. Removable Spray Hood
5. Mooring Ring
6. Lift Handles
7. Ice Runners

color, using a non-reflecting grade finish. Similarly, with a combination fishing-and-hunting boat, painting it some neutral shade of brown or green will simplify seasonal maintenance and camouflage it to a certain extent for hunting.

In any case, ducks get more cautious as the season progresses, and reflections from a boat's glossy paint or varnish, the glint of metal hardware or a motor's chromed parts may spook them more than the actual presence of the boat.

If you don't care to go to the extent of changing your boat's color scheme, you can still make your craft inconspicuous. Gunny sacks, old khaki canvas or commercial camouflage fabric are commonly used, but the material should be cut roughly to size for the parts it is to cover. The motor should be completely shrouded. Some gunners even make rush mats to camouflage their boats. Naturally, a minimum of camouflaging will be required where it is possible to pull the boat into tall grass or rushes and bend them over to conceal it. Always select the thickest clump of grass in the line of flight, working your boat in at right angles to the flight way. A good idea is to steady the boat by securing it with twine from the oarlocks to bundled clumps of grass or reeds.

The bigger role boats play in hunting is not only affording more hunters better sport, but is having the effect of lengthening their season in the outdoors. With the woods and waters offering so much, whether it's gunning on a lonely marsh or floating a creek for varmints, it's as good an excuse as any for using a boat to enjoy a day in the open.

10   Boats for Camping

In DISCUSSING boats and camping, we can find ourselves entangled in something similar to the old chicken-and-egg routine—which came first? Among your outdoor activities, do you place more emphasis on boating or on camping? Assuming your first love to be boating, you'll find you can extend your horizon by including camping.

Camping will give you and your cruising crew the opportunity of stretching legs and spreading out for a night's sleep on solid ground. It can mean more ambitious culinary effort with fires not practical or safe on a boat, and the romance of a blazing campfire at night. All of this can be important after day-long confinement on a small cruiser. If you are restricted to a small runabout by budget or by the waterways you use, camp-cruising may mean the only way you're going to be able to make an overnight trip.

On the other hand, it is obvious that the outdoorsman who limits his recreation to camping can double his pleasure by adding a boat. Just in the sense of extending his camping perimeters, a boat will put him beyond the reaches of his wheels. If he dreams of some enchanted island with complete privacy, he needs a boat.

Besides its atavistic, or back-to-nature appeal, camping has other basic attractions. It can be inexpensive, and it has been made simpler with the development of compact, lightweight equipment and what the food merchants call "convenience foods"—lightweight, dehydrated, and already mixed.

You are missing half of the fun if you don't combine camping and boating.

CAMPING FOR BOATMEN

Small boat cruise camping is an old type of vacationing and weekending, but it's now gaining great new popularity. And despite the fantastic recent growth of boating, most of our waterways remain virtually unchanged. Crowding is largely confined to waters you'd hardly consider for a vacation cruise—those close to big cities and in the more popular resort areas. Even most of our rivers that were once important arteries of transportation have been left behind in the march of progress. Whatever quarter of the nation you live in, you have an almost unlimited choice of small-boat cruising routes.

Any of our fifty-odd larger rivers would provide plenty of distance for the average vacation trip. On most, in fact, you'd travel only a fraction of the length in your allotted time. Many of these rivers originate and lead back into country that's still relatively wild.

Smaller rivers and streams close to home frequently take you into undeveloped country, or at least well away from main highways. They may not be highly scenic, but they appeal to those who like to fish, explore, and move around in a relaxed way. No Camping signs are a rarity. The thoughtful and diplomatic boatman in his contacts with landowners is likely to be told to stay as long as he likes.

As a boat owner, you learn to be as self-sufficient as possible; you prepare yourself and equip your boat against what could happen. When you cruise in a boat, you may be largely on your own, but you generally have no campsite worries. As often as not, the problem is to choose between campsites you see. Moreover, you can assume two things: 1. Provided you follow approved camping practices, you can use the site. 2. If the site is already occupied, you'll likely be asked to land and remain overnight. This joining of other groups, often to travel in company, and the friendliness of the sport generally, play a big part in making camp cruising so popular.

Despite the usual ease of finding campsites, the experienced boat owner goes prepared for any possible shortage. Even a small outboard boat can be arranged and equipped for cooking and sleeping aboard while cruising. Such a set-up is handy on a low-country river with marshy banks. If you're fortunate enough to have a cruising boat with cabin accommodations, all you need is a sheltered spot for dropping anchor overnight.

Most cruising is done in what could be called in-between rigs—fair-size open outboards with a long forward deck and a folding top of some sort, or overnighters with at least a cuddy or small cabin forward and a cockpit shelter. Some kind of overhead protection becomes a necessity on extended cruises. Wind and rain will spoil a trip only slightly quicker than an unrelenting, broiling sun. Then, if need be, you're independent of shore campsites. Perhaps the best practice is to use campsites when they're available, but don't rely on always finding one. When you do find one, you may wish to anchor close in to shore, sleeping aboard, but cooking supper ashore or at least having an evening campfire there. Sometimes you may prefer to pitch a tent and sleep ashore. There's no reason, incidentally, that a campfire built on a reasonably open beach with plenty of water alongside should· be at all dangerous. And often you'll find a ready supply of driftwood close at hand for the fire.

In your advance planning for a small-boat camping cruise, it's wise to try to work out on your chart or map the places you think you'll have to stop for fuel and food. The more independent of the shore you can be, the better. Most cruising boats, by carrying reserve containers, can run two or three days without refueling, and can store enough canned goods and food staples so that only fresh items need be replenished at stopovers. Ice may or may not be obtainable, so it's prudent to learn how to do without. Your biggest problem here—cool drinking water—can be solved with vacuum jugs. Fill the jugs each time you reach a safe supply of pure water. If you're in doubt about the water's purity, be sure to make it safe by using halazone tablets. At the end of this chapter, you'll find a useful tip for helping to solve the ice and drinking water problem.

Your first trip should suit your boating experience, or lack of it. The trip should also suit your general knowledge of the outdoors and of making yourself comfortable in camp. If you own a boat and have used it only on local waters, consider one of our larger rivers or a tributary. Only a few of our popular waterway routes make for hazardous boating. The majority call for only ordinary boating skill and ability to adapt yourself to new conditions.

If, on the other hand, you've always done your camping by car, it's sensible to do your first cruise camping on some short and placid route. Particularly during this learning period, the distance you cover has little to do with the pleasure you get. Quite often some close-to-home river or chain of connecting lakes, ponds, and streams will provide a suitable route of 50 miles or longer, studded with good campsites.

If you have a cruise-camping trip in mind for next season, start your planning early. It's a pleasant way to spend several winter evenings. The various states publish vacation literature that takes in waters of any importance. Check, too, with your local service stations. The larger oil companies publish cruise maps that even a highway dealer should be able to get for you. These maps, while not complete enough for actual navigation, give a general picture of a great variety of water routes.

When you finally narrow your choice to one or two areas, write the state or states involved, addressing the publicity or conservation department at the capital city, and ask if there's any special literature or information on the waterway in question, what books have been written about it, and what special maps—river, topographical, or country—apply, and where you can get them. All of it should enable you to size up quite accurately the route's potential for camping, fishing, and sight-seeing.

The beginner who's looking for a route that's short and easy but still interesting should do his inquiring locally. Your boat-and-motor dealer, if he's a good one, should be able to help. Not only will he know local waters and be able to tell you about possible routes, but he'll likely be glad to put you in touch with outboarding or cruising clubs in the vicinity. The eventual outcome may be that you'll be asked to go along as a guest on one of their overnight cruises. You'll return all the keener on cruise camping, and this bit of experience will help you decide what equipment you'll need or want.

You'll find the more up-and-coming dealers may send boats along on such cruises, taking you as guests with someone along to handle the boat and show you how it's done. While this is a clever sales gimmick from the dealer's standpoint, it gives you a better idea of what cruise camping's all about and may even get you onto the rudiments of boat handling. On the annual cruises that most outboard clubs take, members frequently invite another couple as guests on a share-the-cost basis.

Dealers will often have rigs they'll rent for cruise-camping trips. These are large, used outboard boats with a suitable used motor and likely a matching used trailer. Invariably these rigs are from traded-in stock, but probably reconditioned for resale. It's not likely that a dealer will rent to a rank beginner, but possibly you can get from him sufficient training beforehand to give you enough experience for starting out. Some dealers conduct such training classes themselves; others have arrangements with someone who'll teach you at so much per hour. True, such service is another sales gimmick, but you profit by getting started right. It's amazing how much you can learn in half a dozen such practice periods.

The ideal way, of course, is to follow up such practice with a winter course of lectures and study in small-boat handling and safety. Such courses are conducted pretty much all over the country by organizations like the U.S. Power Squadrons and the Coast Guard Auxiliary. If you must do your learning on your own, take your first trip on some quiet waterway where you'll be away from too many other boats and can make mistakes in reasonable safety.

Often, in building up an outfit, a new owner will buy the boat and motor first, hiring a trailer until he can afford the good one that he has in mind. Many dealers not only rent trailers but also provide a boat-hauling service at so much per mile. This hauling service works well when, instead of making a round trip and ending at your starting point, you travel more or less in one direction and finish up far from where you started.

If you rent a trailer, particularly for long hauls, be sure you get one that's dependable, including its tires. Also see that any chocking or support arrangements are adjusted to fit your boat. Easy loading and unloading features are not too important since you'll only be doing these jobs once and can generally get help.

Another type of rental that's worth investigating is the deal in which you hire practically everything required for the trip, bringing only your personal gear. If you are lucky, perhaps you can arrange to end the trip at some downstream point where the rental agency has a branch. Canoe-outfit rentals have long been popular, and so have guide-conducted float trips. In different areas, outboard-powered houseboats can be rented. But now this chartering or renting of completely equipped live-aboard outboards is a fast-growing business with agencies springing up on more and more popular waterways.

If you own a small outboard boat or a canoe, the only other gear you need to at least try cruise-camping is a minimum camping outfit. Some of the longest trips on record have been made with very simple and inexpensive rigs.

Most cruising couples and family groups, however, prefer a boat of 16 to 20 feet, either a live-aboard model or an open one that can be adequately closed in for sleeping. A typical cabin outboard will sleep two adults comfortably on permanent berths up forward, while two other passengers can sleep in the cockpit, particularly if the seats there convert into bunks. In such a boat, the cabin may have a compact but handy galley and built-in marine toilet. Be sure to check on local laws or regulations regarding use of marine toilets. There is a growing trend to restrict their use on confined waters.

You'll find plenty of storage space on the boat once you've learned to utilize it to best advantage. It's impossible to be definite on cost figures for an outboard outfit of this size, because there's a wide variety in basic quality and extra features. However, the cost of a good complete cruising rig—boat, motor, and trailer—can be kept within the range of a so-called low-priced car, say $2,500. This would allow around $1,200 for the boat, $500 for a motor, and $300 for a trailer, and would still give a $500 leeway for these items and for additional equipment.

Judging by the way rigs of this sort are selling, they're within the budget of a great many families. Such a rig is a sensible buy apart from the pleasure it will give. Boats like this last well and age gracefully. They permit vacation cruises and weekend trips on which, aside from what you spend for fuel, your only outlay will be for sight-seeing and food.

BOATS FOR CAMPERS

Experienced campers, or at least those carrying a boat, will usually agree that a craft of some kind can double the enjoyment of a trip. It's important, however, to select a boat that will be easy to transport and handle out of water and, equally important, one that will do the job in actual water service.

It's easy to sell campers on the advantages of having a boat. By looking around, you can usually see examples of how well the idea has worked out for others. This is especially true if there are children of school age in the family. This is when a boat can help most. Your camping interest is strengthened as you discover side activities made possible by having a boat. It all leads to a keener appreciation of the outdoors.

One big difference that a boat can make is in the kind of campsites used. Campers with boats are more independent about where they set up camp. They're apt to pioneer in their search for more isolated sites and fishing waters. True, they then must pass up the facilities and conveniences of developed public sites. But they enjoy the challenge of being on their own, dependent on their equipment and woodmanship to make themselves comfortable.

Before shopping for a boat, ask yourself these questions: How will I carry the boat? Or should I trailer it? How many persons will I ordinarily want to carry? What will it be used for mostly? How much should I spend?

Be prepared to compromise, especially on size. The job of carrying or towing should not hinder your driving noticeably, and getting the boat into the water and loaded afterwards shouldn't be back-straining jobs. Boats that are a chore to load and unload are never used as often as they might otherwise be. But, despite this stressing of portability, remember that any boat's suitability for a camper's particular service is judged in the water. Easy as it

Auto-top boats present no carrying problem and are big enough to extend your camping range. Boat should be shaped so as to hug the top of the car.

may be to handle a boat ashore, if it's not satisfactory in actual use, you've made a mistake in your selection.

Usually a camper's requirements are served best and most inexpensively by carrying the boat on top of the car or station wagon, or atop a small house trailer or a pickup with demountable house body. Your other logical choice, particularly with a car or wagon, is to use a trailer.

Trailering has certain advantages. For one thing, there's no practical limit to the size boat you can own. Nor, with a suitable trailer, should the launching and loading of even a sizable boat be any greater chore than manhandling a comparatively light craft. Another consideration is that bulky gear, such as tent and sleeping bags, can be carried in the boat. Also, because of the boat's size, the trailer rig may be preferred for uses other than camping, such as fishing trips on fairly open waters.

But, even so, the auto-top boats win out in popularity with car campers. One consideration is that you may not want to invest in a trailer let alone in a boat large enough to require one. Or you may feel that towing a loaded trailer behind your car would be an unnecessary inconvenience. Or you may want to be more independent of developed launching sites, preferring a boat that is truly portable, one that can actually be manhandled or even portaged.

For carrying purposes, the boat should be one that will hug the roof of the vehicle when mounted upside down, offering a minimum of wind resistance. For the mounting, a standard set of crossbar mounts fitted with suction cups will suffice. However, it's wise to have special hold-downs, such as the type with cam-action locks, to hold the boat securely against shifting.

While there is no precise limit to the length and beam of a boat that can be carried this way, nor seldom any question of the vehicle's roof taking the

Light rigs are best for most campers. Boat can be manhandled, even portaged.

load, the maximum weight for such carrying is generally around 100 pounds. Boats of this weight can be loaded and unloaded by two adults without strain. But even so, especially where one must work unaided, a difference of 10 or so is quite noticeable.

If you should have your mind set on a heavier boat, the loading and unloading can be solved by using one of the manufactured carriers designed for the job. These range from a simple rubber roller mounted on the after end of the car's roof to mechanical loaders that permit one person to handle 125-lb. and even heavier boats. Most can be classed as loader-carriers since they also lock the boat in place.

Without such an aid, and keeping within that 100-pound weight limit, one still has a wide choice of boats. In most cases, the simplest way of solving the problem is to buy an auto-top boat. These, generally, have the features needed for car campers. They're light for their size, yet are strongly built. The design affords maximum carrying capacity and stability for the particular length. The boat will be a good all-around performer for its size. It will not be fast under power, but it will take a small motor and be entirely suitable for ordinary fishing and exploring. Naturally, such a boat should be used on

Johnboat is perfect rig for campers who seek isolated fishing waters.

By combining camping with your small-boat cruising, you can enjoy extended trips to remote areas you could not otherwise reach by car or on foot.

small waters, not on bodies big enough to get rough. But that's no great disadvantage to the average camper. All important, the construction will be some leakproof type. Such a boat won't leak despite being repeatedly in and out of the water and exposed to hot sun. Moreover, the hull design or shape is likely to hug the automobile roof.

If this conventional type of auto-top boat doesn't appeal to you, perhaps you'll prefer a craft that can be rowed or paddled. Or it could be that you want one that will be quite fast with a motor. Or you may want greater load capacity or possibly greater seaworthiness than an auto-top boat can provide. There is also the possibility that you'll want a craft that can be carried in a more compact form.

If you want a boat that will row well, check into the better fishing skiffs. Where the conventional auto-top boat tends to be short and beamy, a skiff designed primarily for rowing will be comparatively long and slim with a narrow stern. If it's intended for occasional use with a motor, the stern will be broader. Lengths for our purpose here, run 10 to 12 feet. Construction should be one of the leakproof types, such as aluminum or possibly canvas or fiberglass over very thin planking, to keep the weight down. A few molded-fiberglass skiffs comply with the weight limit, and a well-built panel-plywood craft should stay leak-free if it is sheltered when not in use. Plywood craft can be had in kit form. Ready-cut parts for aluminum kit boats are also available.

If you're interested in paddling, consider a canoe or a kayak. Canoes, catalogued as hunting or trapping models, come in 12- and 13-foot lengths, weighing from 50 pounds up. There are also panel-plywood canoes of similar size and larger available in kit form that come well within our weight limit of 100 pounds, and others of framework construction weighing considerably less. While these short, full-ended canoes are excellent for car carrying, it is also entirely practical to carry a 16-foot canoe. For one thing, you can easily keep within the weight limit. And the long, slim hull of a canoe can be even easier to load and unload than a short, chunky boat. After all, canoes are built for portaging and can be handled by one man.

Others who are interested in paddling often prefer a kayak, despite its limited load-carrying capacity. Or your choice may be influenced by the lower price tags for rigid-type kayaks, including kit offerings. Understandably, a kayak is less stable than a canoe and requires skillful handling. Canoes or kayaks should be chosen only when your main interest is in lightweight and in paddling. A bracket can be used to take a small motor, or you can buy square-end canoes and kayaks. But a conventional auto-top craft will always make a better motorboat.

Some drawbacks of ordinary rigid craft can be avoided by using a craft designed for compact carrying in packed form. You have a wide choice of boats, canoes, and kayaks that fold or collapse for carrying, in addition to rafts and boats that inflate. Here, you should consider the task of unpacking and setting up the boat each time it is used. If you become tempted to avoid this work by leaving the craft set up for carrying, you'll have lost rather than gained from your choice. Such craft work out best only where compactness is the all-important factor. They take up a minimum of space, and the weight will be low for the given size. Also, the package can be lashed to a rack atop the vehicle to save on valuable inside storage space.

Most campers eventually acquire a motor for their boat. This can extend your fishing and exploring range and add interest to your trips. The requirements are simple. Ordinarily, the boat manufacturer's recommendations will be up to 5 h.p. But even a little $2\frac{1}{2}$ or 3 h.p. is likely to suffice. These small craft are easily driven up to a certain speed, say six or seven miles an hour, and using a motor larger than recommended won't increase the speed appreciably. Instead, the boat will then be hard to control, and even unsafe. It is always wise to stay within the manufacturer's horsepower recommendations.

Best type of construction and proper price to pay are difficult to define here. One pretty much sets the other. Naturally, a high-priced offering will have features that can't be provided in a low-priced boat. Still, the economy model may do the job satisfactorily. The sensible plan is to decide what type of craft will suit your purpose best, then start shopping around and pay enough to buy a good boat of that type.

If you are a camper first and a boatman second, and if you're still unsure about what boat to buy for your camping trips, try a low-priced auto-top boat. It can be used as a sort of trial horse. Chances are it will whet your desire for owning something better. You can always sell a conventional small boat or trade it in on a higher-priced one without taking much of a financial beating in bargaining for a better boat.

CAMP-CRUISING TIPS

For the beginners, or for those who have to convince a reluctant wife, there are two nuisances you'll have to cope with and either of them can kill all enthusiasm in a flash. You can't be comfortable for long if you're wet, and even if you're dry, you can be made uncomfortable—even dangerously so—by insects. Prepare for both annoyances. Keep spare dry clothes where they'll be sure to stay dry and take every opportunity along the way to expose clothing and bedding to sun and air to keep it fresh and dry. Use mosquito netting when you can, but always have a supply of insect repellant for skin application and an aerosol "bug-bomb."

Some campers, especially those who hoof it with a pack on the back, pride themselves on going light. You can do this too—sleeping on spruce boughs, under a blanket of blue. On the other hand, if you have the inclination and the space to indulge it, there are homelike insect-proof tents and folding cots, air mattresses and down-filled sleeping bags. However you choose to do it, the important thing is to do it, and with just a few precautions to avoid disappointment.

Many experienced campers prefer to take along a grill of heavy gauge wire or iron, doing their cooking on an open fire and then enjoying the blaze of an evening campfire. Others prefer to cook on shore with the quick and easy little gas or propane stoves.

If you can, take drinking water from home. Even if you have an opportunity to replenish your supply from perfectly good sources enroute, change of water can do a lot to upset finicky city stomachs, and possibly spoil the trip. One well-used trick is to fill waxed milk cartons with water from home, freeze them and use to keep your ice chest cold. As the water melts, you have a ready supply of good, cold drinking water.

Don't get trapped into the romantic notion that you can eat off the land. Any fish you catch or berries you pick should be considered an added treat—don't count on them.

Don't rely on cardboard boxes to serve as anything but very temporary make-shift pack boxes. Even then, you'll have to protect them—they can't stand much moisture or much of a beating. When they begin to disintegrate, you'll have a mess—armloads of loose groceries and utensils. Those who camp often develop their own wooden grub boxes—some are ingeniously tailor-made to hold selected items and to fit a specific area in the boat. In time, you may want to do the same yourself.

Provide a flashlight for each member of the group—little campers included. It will give a psychological sense of security and it's a practical way of insuring adequate light for any emergency.

A ground-cloth for sitting and sleeping on the ground will repel chilling dampness underneath, and when thrown over your gear will keep out spray and rain from above.

11 Boats for Fishing

THE RIGHT fishing boat makes a big difference in how much you enjoy your sport. Whether you fish the confined waters of a small pond, the larger lakes and rivers, or tackle open stretches of salt water, the right boat guarantees you more comfort and convenience, and often more fish. What's right for one man's fishing, of course, may not be so good for another's. The problem is to pick out the boat that will be best for the kinds of fishing you have in mind. Local preferences can be a good guide.

On small, sheltered waters, bigger boat might be a nuisance.

SMALL BOATS FOR SMALL WATERS

For fishing confined waters—ponds, small lakes, and winding streams—a boat that's too big can be a nuisance. On such waters you want a boat that's easily maneuvered, behaves well at low speeds, and which can be rowed, paddled, or poled if necessary. If you use a trailer, the easier the boat is to unload and reload the better. The same goes for auto-top carrying. But in seeking a boat that's easy to launch and reload, cut down on beam rather than length, and choose a craft of lightweight but leakproof construction. Length is important: with too short a boat you must be always intent on not hooking your fishing partner.

The popular johnboat, in wood or aluminum, comes in a range of sizes.

Canoes, johnboats, long and rather low-sided skiffs, and modern all-purpose hunting boats make excellent two-man fishing craft for confined waters. Right now canoes and johnboats are in good demand, possibly because of a wider choice of models and constructions.

The canoe enthusiast can choose from aluminum, canvas-covered wood, and fiberglass models. Also panel-plywood canoes are low-priced as canoes go, especially if assembled from a kit or built from plans. Other popular small-water boats are those ultralight craft that combine canoe, kayak, and hunting-skiff characteristics.

Still another consideration in the field of boats for confined waters is the wider choice and lower prices of inflatable craft. Though they aren't easy to row and also make poor motorboats, they're quite stable and safe to fish from. They work out best for toting to out-of-the-way waters that can't be reached by car. Their low cost makes them attractive as a sportsman's extra boat.

BEST BOAT FOR OPEN WATERS

If you're considering a boat for less sheltered waters such as larger rivers and lakes, size and speed are important.

Generally speaking, too big a boat will work out better than one that's too small. It will be more comfortable to fish from, particularly with others along, and you can stay out longer. Size makes for seaworthiness. With a 15-foot or longer outboard, you'll be able to fish on days when smaller boats will hardly venture out.

Speed then becomes not only a convenience but a safety factor. By heeding sky warnings and using your boat's speed you can reach shelter before the wind strikes.

Even on windy days you can often use your reasonably large and fast boat. On a fair-size lake, for example, you can possibly skirt along its weather shore, running a much longer distance than you ordinarily would, but reaching reasonably calm water under the protection of the opposite shore. And once you've found what your boat will or won't do safely, you may—if you don't mind taking the beating—make a quick run straight across to such shelter.

Another important point is that larger outboard boats lend themselves to outfitting with fishing features. I'd select a boat for its functional qualities, rather than its flashy appearance.

BIG BOATS FOR BIG WATERS

For still more open waters—large lakes, exposed bays, and around coastal inlets and off beaches—size is vitally important and must be coupled with seaworthiness. Fortunately, there's getting to be a much wider choice of really able big outboards in fishing models, and boat manufacturers have kept pace with the growing popularity of stern-drive power with an amazing range of trailerable big-water stern-drive boats.

All of these larger fishing models are considerably deeper than the conventional outboard. This means that the hull will have a better hold in the water and steering will be easier, especially in a wind. The fishing boat's hull, being deeper, permits a sharper forefoot than can be given the conventional hull, so you avoid undue pounding when bucking a head sea. As compared to the ordinary run of big outboard boats, the topsides forward will have more flare. While this cuts down on space within the boat, the advantage of so much flare is that the boat won't plunge so deeply when encountering big waves. And most of the spray thrown at such times should be deflected rather than being blown over or into the boat to drench its crew.

Largely because such a boat is easier on its crew and on itself, speed can be maintained long after wave conditions have forced a conventional boat to slow down. Often you can fish when other boats must leave for shelter.

It doesn't matter so much what material is used. What's important is how it's used. To play safe here, just remember that the true measure of how a boat is likely to stand up in harder-than-usual service is the experience of its manufacturer and his reputation for building boats for fishing exposed waters.

A forward deck and windshield are common big-boat features. But for fishing use, the deck shouldn't come too far back and the windshield must be functional. Waves will mount the deck to test its staunchness, and you'll use it plenty as a handhold when the boat's pitching. Narrow side decks aren't a bad idea so long as they're not cluttered with fittings. If it's practicable to have the cockpit floor high enough above the water to be made tight and fitted with drains to carry off any water shipped, that's an excellent safety feature.

The stern layout is particularly important to both fishing efficiency and safety. The stern or transom of an outboard boat should prevent waves astern from getting into the boat proper. The big advance in this direction is the long-shaft motor which avoids the need of notching the transom so deeply.

Even with the usual self-draining motor compartment, a long shaft lifts the engine's powerhead that much clearer of the water.

Some of the larger outboard fishing boats even have sterns designed so that the motor or motors, in a properly ventilated compartment, are low enough to be covered by flush hatches. Then with dock-line hawseholes in the deck, permitting installation of stern cleats inside the cockpit, the entire after end of the boat can be kept clear of obstructions that might snag a fish-line.

It's sensible to have a folding shelter over the driver's seat forward, but it should allow him perfect visibility both ahead and astern. In most types of open-water fishing, his handling of the boat is a key factor in the success or failure of the fishing expedition.

In addition to better availability of factory-built fishing boats, there's progress in many coastal areas toward developing husky boats suitable for local conditions. Such builders usually build to order, or supply just the local demand, so you must visit them to make your arrangements. There are also kits that will produce a good basic hull that can be finished for fishing use. And there's an increase in both the number and quality of building plans offered for the man who can build his own sizable fishing boat or who can interest some small builder in turning out at least the bare hull.

Still another new development in this field is promised by the success of catamaran (twin-hulled) craft. During recent years, they've demonstrated their seaworthiness and speed in long-distance racing events over rough-water courses. There's a great flurry in building catamarans of various sizes. They're stable and extremely roomy, and when properly fitted out good ones make fine fishing boats. But here again, hull shape is important, and you should do any buying from a manufacturer whose boats have a good reputation in this field.

Even though you don't expect to encounter truly rough water, a boat that will handle it if need be is always a sensible buy. Chances are you'll become interested in fishing further and further afield. This stepping up to larger waters is helping make the fishing picture what it is. Except for those small confined waters that we talked about at the beginning of this chapter, any large outboard or stern-drive boat of the plainly finished but well-built fishing or utility type is worth the extra it may cost. Its maintenance will be comparatively simple, and these boats are remarkably long-lived. Important, too, from the investment standpoint: they age gracefully. With nothing freakish about their design, they keep on having a high trade-in or resale value.

In addition to its great utility as a boat for fishing, there is nothing wrong with a boat of this general type for most other uses with family or friends. True, such a craft may lack some eye appeal, but this is more than offset by hidden qualities of design and construction. A would-be buyer should also remember what the figures show: chances are four to one that any boat will eventually be used by its owner for fishing.

If your local fishing waters are shallow or rock-strewn, you should investigate jet power—available in both outboard and inboard versions. Lacking

Boat this size can cross rough water to work sheltered shore.

propellers and other underwater projections, they can negotiate a rapids like a goat on a shale slide.

Once you have your fishing boat, the main considerations are proper fitting out. Fishing requires a minimum of special equipment—if you want it that way. But most fishermen take pride in doing what they can to improve their boats. Even a small one can be improved in various ways, and with a large fishing type you can really go all out. Fortunately, having your boat suitably fitted out isn't entirely a matter of spending money. The best fish-taking rigs have resulted largely from their owners using their ingenuity and good judgment—spending their money wisely rather than lavishly.

Big, fast rig can tackle open water, beat squalls to shore.

HOW TO RIG YOUR BOAT FOR FISHING

A good fishing boat is even better when you rig it for exactly the kind of fishing you have in mind. And whether your boat is fresh from the dealer's showroom or you've owned it for several years, there are probably several ways you can make it more efficient.

Small trolling motor can be mounted to one side and low. This mount will tilt.

For trolling or in emergencies, you can use homemade bracket for spare motor.

Of major importance is the way you decide to power the boat. If your boat is a small one—under 12 feet—keep well within the maximum horsepower the manufacturer recommends for it. If you'll be fishing only confined waters, high speed will seldom be important. You might be wise to use a motor that's smaller than usual for such a boat. Then you can operate it most of the time at about the speed where it behaves best. Even for slow trolling a small motor is likely to turn fast enough to run very smoothly.

Where a variety of small waters are concerned, it's wise to investigate electric trolling motors. These can often be used on small waters where gasoline outboards are barred. There also is quite a variety of mechanical propulsion devices, most of them designed for one-arm operation and with the needs of small-boat fishermen in mind.

If your fishing boat is around 12 to 14 feet—the most popular size for use on rivers and other fair-size waters—you want a motor that's powerful enough to drive your boat up to its top speed, yet will behave well when throttled down for long periods of trolling. Motors for boats in this bracket range up to 25 h.p. Many motors in this group have refinements appealing to fishermen, and the larger ones have most of the big-motor features. All of them give good trolling performance.

If your fishing boat is in the top-size bracket, it's probably designed to take plenty of power. And while it's possible to overpower such a boat, too small an engine is more likely to be the cause of any unsatisfactory behavior in a modern big outboard boat.

The bigger your outfit, the more your power plant depends on factors other than the motor. Your fuel system must include adequate tankage, and precautions must be taken against fuel-system failures. Batteries must be properly housed, connected, and maintained. The motor's steering and control systems must be of an approved sort, and correctly laid out and installed.

To have a large or medium-size outboard rig adequately powered, one or two moves may be advisable: 1. Use two motors instead of one. 2. Install the motor (or motors) and all its accessories (fuel tanks, remote controls, and so on) as permanently as practicable.

Remote controls for steering, gearshift, and throttle must be positive-acting and as troubleproof as possible. Permanent installation helps assure such performance. Similarly, any battery must be properly installed. Most of us with big outboards are becoming more and more dependent on electrical power, so a motor that has a suitable generator or alternator can be a big boon to convenience and safety by keeping a battery charged while the boat is under way.

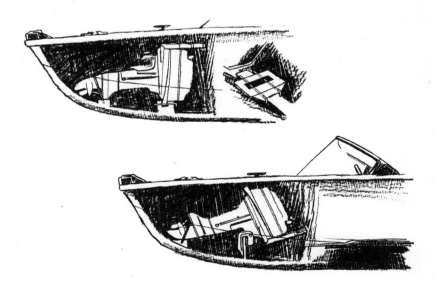

Spare motor can be carried securely in bow (top). Detail shows block, pins that hold carrying handle. Another way to hold spare motor is to use transom clamp on crosswise board (bottom).

Many of today's outboard fishing boats are so big that they require two top-size motors in order to develop top speed. Or a pair may be used to improve the boat's maneuverability. On boats that are not quite so large, many fishermen prefer to use two motors of conservative size rather than a single big one. Despite extra expense and some power loss, two motors halve your chances of being caught without power. And when trolling with only one of these motors running, you needn't throttle down nearly as much as you'd have to with a big motor.

Another popular two-motor set-up is to use a single motor for normal running, and carry a small motor for trolling and emergency use. A 5-h.p. job, even a good used one, will answer these purposes. Fit floor chocks, preferably under the forward deck, where this small auxiliary motor can be fastened securely. Often, a small motor bracket installed well down on one side of the transom is required to give the small motor's propeller its proper bite in the water (see illustrations).

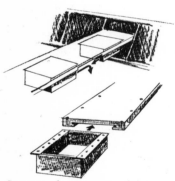

Waterproof boxes of metal, or plywood that's fiberglassed, can be fitted to underseat space; hold bait, fish, ice.

Drawers for storage slide on strips of brass, and move lengthwise under seat.

Whether your boat is small or large, another vital factor for successful fishing is to arrange the interior properly. The secret is to keep your extra equipment simple and light. Buy your larger pieces of equipment to fit into unused spaces, such as those under seats.

Make good use of shock cord, which is strong, yet flexible. It's fine for slinging oars and rods under the gunwales. Also, suitable lengths fitted with S-hook ends can be used for holding down bulkier gear (see illustration).

To keep tackle and small things orderly, you may want to install easy-to-make drawers under the seats. An even easier move is merely to make shock-cord slings for the underseat storage of tackle boxes and the like (see illustrations). Waterproof bags or pouches for suspending inside the gunwales put small things within easy to reach, and they can be carried home.

In a small boat, the seating can often be improved for fishing. If a cushion won't give a comfortable sitting height, an extra seat top may do the

With harness made of shock cord, bulky gear can be held in place.

Gas can that isn't permanently installed can be anchored with shock cord.

Shock cord makes a quick sling to hold a tackle box.

trick. Sometimes it's removable, but more often the space between the two is filled with boxlike drawers. Another possibility is the clamp-on folding chair. Some of them swivel or can be adjusted for height.

For safety's sake it's a good idea to have rowlocks installed where they will make rowing easiest in an emergency, and to carry light, good-quality oars of the right length for your boat.

Of more importance to the fisherman than to the ordinary big-boat owner are the anchor, its line, and any mechanical means of handling them. There's a wide choice of makes and types, and the trick is to find one that's right for your particular fishing. Many experienced fishermen carry two anchors: 1. A patent type with say 100 feet of ½-inch Manila or nylon line. 2. A small mushroom or drag.

Where the bottom is snag-infested, it's a good idea to carry a trip line and buoy. The ¼-inch line should be plenty long enough to reach bottom. One end is tied to the crown of the anchor, the other to a small wood float. If the anchor gets jammed, a straight pull on the trip line will almost invariably free it.

Stowing an anchor and its tackle is important. Keep it out of the way, but always ready.

Aim for good footing within your boat. If bottom frames are exposed, floor racks or slats will help you avoid tripping over them. See that they're clipped down securely. Floor surfaces should be finished with nonskid paint.

With more and more outboard and stern-drive boats fishing in big waters, two features that are becoming more popular are outriggers and rod holders. The outriggers are likely to be aluminum (possibly telescoping) or fiberglass, and 15 to 18 feet long. Rubber liners for sockets can be had, or an aluminum pole may be bushed with fiberglass to cut noise and pole wear.

Rod holders also come in various styles, some being combination rod and outrigger-pole holders. Some are intended to be fastened to a fishing chair or a cockpit box.

Special fishing chairs, while not essential, are handy when you're fighting big fish. Small-boat models are available at attractive prices. If you plan to use more than one such chair in your boat, arrange them to give the lines a good spread, and also to leave working space between chairs and along the sides and stern of the boat.

Would you like a built-in bait or fish well? They're fine if you can find the space and they don't leak. To have the well leakproof, build it of plywood and line with fiberglass. Where a permanent installation is impractical, you might be able to use a removable type, putting it in by connecting its hose clamps to hull fittings and taking it out by disconnecting its hose clamps and plugging the hull fittings. Any outlets such as this should have rubber flaps outside to keep out the surge of water. Still another type is a box-like affair that hangs to one side over the transom. If bait or fish well can serve also as a seat, so much the better (see illustration). Sometime a fish box has a section bulkheaded off to hold ice, and perhaps in this section you can keep beverages and perishable food.

A fishing boat, of course, is more likely than others to be out in rainy and rough weather, so don't overlook a dependable method of keeping your boat clear of water. Stern bailers or automatic drains operate satisfactorily when the boat is moving right along, but a sizable fishing boat should also have a convenient and effective bilge pump.

Tackle boxes should be handy, but sheltered from the weather and spray. Carry spare tackle in a separate box or drawer that's kept stored. Still another drawer or box can hold such fishing tools as wire-cutting pliers, small screwdrivers, reel wrenches, reel lubricant, plastic friction tape, and ferrule cement. Racks or strap holders should be provided to keep unused rods from under foot.

Since you may be cruising for hours out of sight of land, and fog is always a potential hazard, you should have a good compass properly installed.

None of the electronic navigation or communication aids can make up for lack of basic knowledge in how to use a compass and charts. However, for the owner of a big boat who has mastered the rudiments of finding his way about on the water, electronic equipment of this sort can help in mastering the finer points. And certain equipment can be truly advantageous in your fishing. The electronic depth-sounding devices are the best example.

They indicate deep holes, rocks, or old wrecks where fishing may be productive, and similarly help you relocate a good fishing spot. There are two main types: 1. The depth indicators, which flash the depth on a dial. 2. The recorders, which produce a graph on a tape. The depth indicators are moderately priced, and have become so popular they're often called fish finders.

Increased use of transistors has made it possible to produce smaller electronic units which require less space and less power to operate. Compact radiotelephones have been very much a part of the small-boat scene for several years. Now it is both possible and practical for small-boat operators to equip their craft with dependable electronic navigation and piloting aids. As the market for this equipment has increased, the prices have come down. Some units are available in kit form. If you can handle a soldering iron and can follow directions, these offer good winter-evening projects and save you the high cost of labor.

Obviously you could spend a great amount of money if you rigged your fishing boat with everything that's available. On the other hand, there's a lot that you can do to improve your boat for fishing while staying with small or moderate outlays. Part of the fun of owning a fishing boat is that you can always be planning at least one more way to improve it.

12 Buying a Boat

BEFORE BUYING a boat, size up your particular situation. Investigate the waters you expect to fish and select a boat to suit the conditions. Or, if you have your mind set on a certain boat, limit its use to waters that are in keeping with the boat's size and seaworthiness. If you're doubtful about how large a boat you want, buy one that may be too large rather than too small. If it's motor's size you're doubtful about, reverse this thinking and keep well within the boat manufacturer's recommendations.

Don't overpower or overload any boat. Put off taking out friends until you get to know your boat and have acquired some experience. Avoid standing up in a small boat and be careful in moving about in a larger one.

Read what you can in boating and try to apply pertinent advice. Observe how experienced boatmen manage their craft. As you acquire confidence in yourself and your boat, any fear of water will gradually be lost and be replaced by a healthy respect for it.

The belief that boating is costly is not necessarily true. And, certainly, it needn't be so as far as the average sportsman is concerned.

This is one sport you can get into in a very small way, if need be, and still have fun. It also is one in which you can progress and still keep your investment low. And if you use your boat for fishing, hunting, or camping trips, you have several cost advantages over the average pleasure-boat owner.

Aside from incidentals, there are a couple of other cost items that you may or may not want to figure into your boating budget: depreciation and interest on your investment. Most of us disregard the latter, feeling that the enjoyment we get from the boat more than justifies the amount of money tied up in it. Depreciation, however, can best be kept low by buying a boat with which you'll remain satisfied, and spending enough to get a quality product that will last well. Trading in during the first year or so of a boat's life is an expensive practice. After that, depreciation more or less levels off, especially on the utility type.

The bigger the boat the more it costs, and, in theory at least, the larger the boat the more expensive it is to operate and maintain. But you'll probably use a larger boat more because you can make it really comfortable by using such extras as a demountable top, removable seat backs, and cushions. If there's a forward deck or small cabin, you can install a small marine toilet and possibly build a compact galley or even a couple of seats that could be converted into bunks.

The bigger the boat, the drier and more comfortable it is likely to be in rough water, and it should be able to maintain its speed better than a small one. But, whatever the size of the boat, it is always advisable to stick to its manufacturer's recommendations regarding horsepower. The boat will be designed to be safe at a certain top speed. Using a motor with horsepower greater than suggested won't increase that speed. Instead you chance making an ordinarily well-behaved boat difficult to manage and unsafe at high speeds.

Favor the fisherman or utility models rather than flashy runabouts or the de luxe models. If possible, confine yourself to standard makes represented by reliable dealers, and take advantage of what has been done to improve boats from the maintenance standpoint. Whether the boat you favor is made of fiberglass, aluminum, wood, or plywood, be sure it is well-built.

The larger boat, of course, will require more power. But for fishing, you can afford to be conservative. It's best to keep well within the manufacturer's power recommendations. Unless you really need them, don't order side features or extras.

Beyond this, the materials, and design of the modern, big outboard or stern-drive boat tends to keep the cost of ownership down. In glass, aluminum, and wood, great strides have been made to provide boats which require remarkably little maintenance beyond being kept clean. Unlike a fancy, highly stylized runabout, a fisherman or utility version will retain its value much better over the years. Because of this longer life, the original cost of the boat and equipment can be thought of as a long-term investment.

What about insurance, financing, and storage? The cost of these things should be considered, but each owner's case is different.

If you finance the purchase of your rig, it will undoubtedly be insured as part of the arrangement. There is nothing wrong with buying a properly selected rig on time. Quite often, a package deal offers a boat, motor, essential equipment, and even a trailer at a price substantially lower than you would pay for each item purchased separately. This saving can be used to cover the cost of financing.

You should insure in proportion to the risk involved. You can check with responsible owners of rigs such as the one you have in mind to find out what they are carrying. If you can't get reliable information, put yourself in the hands of a reputable agent.

Experienced owners have learned that it's a good idea to keep maintenance in mind when they are shopping around for a boat. They know, for example, that a plainly finished craft, which is preferred for fishing or camping, will require far less upkeep than a de luxe version of the same model. A fancy paint job involving several colors will slow up repainting and increase cost. White paint is more easily maintained than dark colors. In hot weather, if the boat is wood, white paint will help keep seams tight and guard against

This type of simple rig has improved in quality and dominates the rental field.

rot. Don't be too impressed by claims made that certain boats are virtually maintenance free. The extent to which this applies depends largely on how the manufacturer has used and finished the material. Excellent progress has been made in this direction, but the reputation of the manufacturer and the price of the boat still largely determines what will apply.

Where and how to keep your boat are important. A boat kept in a dirty location will need more attention than one stored in a clean area. Polluted water can rot wood, and marsh gas can mottle white surfaces and fade colors. Soot-laden air makes frequent washings necessary, and too many washings with strong detergents can quickly break down any finish.

Keeping your boat on a trailer in your driveway should avoid getting it dirty. If you shelter the craft with a lightweight cover, so much the better. For outdoor storage, where the boat is likely to be set on a cradle, use a heavier winter cover. Such a cover should be put over a framework or padding to avoid chafe, and the entire structure designed to drain rain and not hold too much snow. Actually, maintenance cost and effort can be cut enough in this way to eventually cover the expense of such a shelter.

Angler cuts fuel expense by using big motor for long runs and small motor (note raised prop) for short runs, trolling.

Where a boat will be kept in the water, it's wise to seek a location that's both clean and convenient to good fishing and attractive boating waters. Chances are storage facilities will be found in the vicinity. However, if you have your own place on the water, or possibly access to a suitable site, you can put in your own small dock with boat shelter and hoist, using the do-it-yourself equipment now available.

You can also keep the cost of operating a big outboard down by buying a small second motor, possibly a good, used job. Using the small motor gives you cheap running while on the fishing grounds, especially when trolling. The second motor also provides a safety margin. The small motor will get you back to the dock should the large one fail. Some boatmen use two motors of equal power to provide this safety factor, but this arrangement is more expensive. For ordinary cruising, one large motor uses less gasoline than two of equal power. For most outboarders, the best solution is one large motor plus a smaller auxiliary.

Operating costs for any boat can be kept down by powering it conservatively and using its power intelligently. But you should be satisfied with the speed that affords the best all-round efficiency. This usually means operating at three-quarter throttle. An engine powerful enough to drive a boat at its top cruising speed, but run at three-quarter throttle, will be more economical to run than a smaller engine that almost always must be operated with the throttle wide open. In cases where the cost of operating a large outboard motor may be prohibitive, a stern-drive outfit, a four-cycle inboard, or even a small diesel might be a good solution.

Ratios of power to weight favor gasoline engines over diesels. There is a wider variety of gasoline engines to choose from—readily available and at lower prices. The necessary fuel, proper replacement parts, and mechanics familiar with their repair are relatively easy to find.

However, a diesel engine has a much more economical appetite. It will go farther on a gallon of fuel and its fuel is a lot cheaper. From a safety standpoint, the fuel doesn't give off an explosive vapor. Ruggedness, dependability and fuel economy makes the diesel a favorite for arduous service.

PAY AS YOU GO

The installment purchase of boats is now considered about as logical and proper as the credit buying of cars and household items. Keep in mind, however, that while very low down payments and long contracts may be initially attractive, they can appreciably boost the total cost of your outfit.

Remember, too, that a personal loan from a bank is quite different from borrowing from the so-called small-loan places. A small-loan company's rate of interest can be high.

If, instead of going to your own bank, you get your credit from the dealer, your contract will be according to a plan worked out by his banker or possibly by some large manufacturer whose products he sells. Naturally there'll be a down payment, and monthly payments to cover the balance. One third down, and eighteen to twenty-four months for the balance can be considered standard practice. Some plans, however, require a down payment as low as 10 percent and allow you up to three years for the balance. Interest will likely be at 6 percent. There aren't likely to be any hidden charges although you will undoubtedly have to carry insurance on the outfit and pay for insurance on your life for the term of the loan.

The red tape you must go through before you can actually get your boat will vary. Plans with a minimum of red tape are on the increase.

Some dealers will merely phone your credit information to their banks, and complete the entire transaction on the spot. More often, though, the bank will make a routine check of your record, just as in any other loan transaction. In addition, if the amount involved warrants it, some inquiries may be made into your experience with boats and your reputation for financial responsibility.

The boat or equipment you buy becomes security for the loan, of course, and that's why you're required to have insurance.

Bear in mind, too, that you will have to maintain the boat as well as meet those monthly payments. Regardless of the amount of interest or carrying charges, the aggregate cost on a long-term loan will be far larger than on a short one.

In your enthusiasm for the new boat, you won't begrudge the first few monthly payments. But after six months, or certainly a year, much will depend on whether the boat is "right" for you. Are you sure that the boat is entirely suitable for the use you have in mind? And after you've finished paying for the boat, will its type, design, and construction still make it good property? These points are important enough if you're paying cash, but even more so if you're buying on time. If you continue satisfied with the boat, you won't mind pinching in other directions to make the payments.

Just as you shop around for the best buy in a boat, you should also shop around for the best possible credit terms. Interest rates of the lending agencies will vary across the country and even within the same city. Of various plans offered, compare the toal amount you eventually will have paid for your boat.

BUYING A USED RIG

You, the buyer, are the main factor in determining whether or not the purchase of a used boat will prove to be a wise investment. You can always get professional assistance in checking out the soundness of a used rig, but a great deal will depend on how much reconditioning you'll have to do to put the outfit into serviceable shape.

You'll find that this market isn't as orderly as the used-car business. Prices are less standardized, and there may be some bargaining involved. But while there's a limit to what can be done by the average buyer to improve a used car, there's no limit on what can be done to make a sound used boat almost as good as new. It means work, of course, and the big question is how much of it you are in a position to do.

Before taking the trouble to look at a used boat, try to find out its make. If an ad or a dealer's listing mentions the manufacturer's name, that's a good sign. Don't waste time examining a boat of unknown or questionable manufacture. But one that bears the name of a nationally known manufacturer is generally worth considering.

If you're satisfied with the make, and the boat is the right size and type for you, then consider what condition it is in and the price being asked for it. There is a point of condition beyond which, however low the price may be, a boat must be considered a poor buy. With small, simple craft, condition should be quite apparent. It is not easy to conceal serious defects in them.

What, if anything, is wrong with the boat? How much work will be involved in putting it into shape? Don't worry about the cost of materials if all the boat needs is a refinishing job. But how about your capability and facilities for doing the work?

It is easy to be too ambitious in a project of this sort. Naturally, the amount you've budgeted for buying a used rig will get you a much bigger boat than if you were buying a new one. It's also easy to be led astray by offerings which, for their size, seem low-priced. But from the average buyer's standpoint, with large outboards, stern drives, and small inboards, there should be only surface or finish defects to be corrected. This, in itself, could keep a spare-time worker busy all winter. Reconditioning a boat requires the willingness to learn, to work carefully, and to improve your ability as you go along.

Often, a two to four-year-old boat that has been neglected will look particularly seedy. Varnished surfaces will be down to the bare wood, the wood may be weather-stained, paint will be badly checked and flaking off in places, metal trim may be loose, and bilges undoubtedly will be filthy. Some dealers do a quick reconditioning job on such trade-ins. Others, because of the labor involved, prefer to sell them as they are. These badly run-down boats are often good buys if they are priced right and if the neglect hasn't caused the main and framework members to rot or deteriorate. There's less chance of finding concealed faults in one of these run-down boats than in a reconditioned craft. With the wood more or less bare, it's easy to detect any. If a fair amount of money is involved, call in a yacht surveyor or an experienced professional to check out the rig for you. The money spent for his services would not only be good insurance against going wrong, but you'll get advice on whether the boat's condition is in keeping with your ability to recondition it.

The equipment situation tends to make used boats attractive, particularly large outboards and inboards. When looking over such offerings, find out just what equipment goes with the boat and is included in the price. Most such boats are turned in more or less completely equipped. Today, an owner's investment in a new boat can easily represent 40 percent for extras.

Don't attempt to be an expert on engines. Call in a competent service man or a marine mechanic. You want two opinions from him. First, on the mechanical condition of the engine, second, whether only a tune-up is required or a complete reconditioning.

In all, carefully balance the work, cash outlay, and the risk involved against the saving you estimate you'll make by buying a used rig rather than a comparable new one. Remember that there are few downright bargains in this used-boat market. Where used boats give complete satisfaction, and plenty do, it's because the owner bought intelligently and depended on competent outside advice in addition to spending plenty of time on reconditioning his rig.

RENTING BEFORE PURCHASE

If you are unable to make up your mind about the type and size of boat to buy, you might try renting. By patronizing several places to try out a variety of boats, you can crystallize your thinking. Similarly, if you are thinking of buying a sizable boat, you can gain experience beforehand by chartering a boat of the type and size you have in mind. You'll also learn whether a boat of that type will suit your purpose as well as you suppose.

Boat liveries handling outboard skiffs and rowboats have long been a familiar fixture at fishing resorts. If you are interested in this size range, modern liveries ordinarily charge from $1.50 to $5 for a full day. With a motor, the daily rate may be from $6 to $15, depending on the size of boat and motor. Usually, rates are lower on weekdays and in more remote sections. Some liveries require a deposit of around $10.

The boat should be clean, tight, and safe. It being a rental craft shouldn't be too apparent. There should be the necessary equipment, not only the required buoyant cushions but an anchor and rope, oars or a paddle, and enough gas to more than take you where you're going and back. Some liveries on open waters supply their customers with a chart or map.

Most drive-it-yourself agencies operate on the assumption that if you can drive a car you can quickly learn to operate an outboard. Surprisingly, this privilege is rarely abused and these places seem able to operate without boats being badly damaged. You are, of course, started out right. An attendant will show you how to start and operate the motor, taking you for a trial run to familiarize you with the boat. This also gives him a chance to size up your capability at handling the rig. If you pass muster, you'll be cautioned to stay close to shore or at least keep in protected waters and avoid exposing yourself to heavy traffic. If you're totally inexperienced and the attendant is dubious about your learning quickly, the agency may insist on your taking a skipper, at an extra charge, for at least your first trip. This may also apply if you want to fish offshore or where conditions are dangerous. However, if you're anxious to gain experience, such personal instruction is worth the extra cost.

If you want a larger rig than the average livery provides, you'll find

If you can drive a car, you can learn to handle this drive-it-yourself rental.

drive-it-yourself boat agencies in many areas along the Atlantic and Pacific coasts. The range is from 16-foot open outboards to 28-foot stern-drive and inboard cruisers. Most of the cruisers have bunks, toilet, and a small galley. If the livery caters largely to fishermen, boats will have a bait tank, fish box, rod holders,and possibly outriggers.

Naturally, rates vary with the size of boat and the section of the country. They're likely to be less on weekdays, and discounted even more late in the season.

Where a larger boat, over 30 feet for example, is wanted, charter rather

Charter craft offer services of captain and mate. Most accommodate six anglers.

Renting a houseboat offers mobility, and it costs no more than leasing a cottage.

than hire. While some individual owners charter direct, most prefer to list the boat with a yacht broker who handles the details. You make your arrangements with him.

More and more boat owners nowadays are anxious to charter for a few weeks during the boating season to help defray their maintenance and other costs.

You should, of course, determine before signing up just what the rate includes. Usually, it covers the broker's fee and possibly delivery, but not fuel, food, and side expenses. For most charter boats, up to 45 feet for example, one is his own captain. If you're inexperienced, and for larger boats, a captain is taken on at a rate approximately 50 percent higher. The quality of the boat as well as the size will have its effect, but it is not unusual for a power cruiser or auxiliary sailboat sleeping four persons to charter for around $250 a week. But above the 32-foot size, charter rates usually climb rapidly.

13 Your Choice of Power

THE OPTIONS available for powering your boat continue to increase; the combinations multiply. It is no longer a simple decision of inboard or outboard power—which used to be pretty much determined by the size of the boat. Now you have a choice of outboard motor with its portability or at least removability, inboard engine with fixed shaft and propeller, and the increasingly popular combination of the two—the inboard-outboard (I/O).

The I/O has muscled its way into the breach between what used to be the small-sized inboard boat and the large-sized outboard boat.

Ideal power for small boats (say up to 16 feet) is going to remain the exclusive domain of the ubiquitous outboard motor. Keen competition among the manufacturers of outboard motors has assured us a high level of quality. Sophisticated engineering long ago produced dependability, and it continues to develop refinements which give the owner push-button starting, fingertip control and almost noiseless operation—in a full range of sizes.

But for boats from 16 to 26 feet in length—and consequently those in the upper end of the trailerable range—you may be faced with a puzzling choice between a large outboard, an inboard-outboard, or a conventional inboard. True, the inboard may be impractical in your case, but you must understand the principle of inboard propulsion to appreciate what has been done in developing the inboard-outboard as a compromise type.

Modern, 18-foot utility with conventional outboard motor . . .

... compared with 18-footer and its inboard-outboard motor.

For some potential boat owners, the disadvantages of the inboard are the exposed hull appendages—the strut, shaft, rudder, and propeller. These determine the boat's draft, and they are highly vulnerable to damage in shallow water. The inboard also requires special facilities for loading and launching and a special trailer for hauling. In contrast, the inboard-outboard combines these drive parts in a single stern unit which functions like an outboard motor. The outboard unit is raised for launching, loading and beaching. Operation, handling, and trailering is the same as that of an outboard motor of comparable size and weight.

Next, how much do you care to spend? An inboard-outboard will cost more than an outboard rig of comparable size and quality. One typical 19-foot fiberglass runabout with 110 h.p. outboard motor lists from $3,395.60. The same hull with 110 h.p. inboard-outboard lists for $4,095. Your comparison may not be that simple. You may be considering different boats with different optional power.

To make a comparison, add the cost of a suitable outboard motor to the price of the outboard boat model. Now consider the extras. A good outboard is likely to come fully equipped, but there will still be certain controls and electrical equipment to buy and install. Also, you may find that a 12-gallon fuel tank, while standard equipment on the inboard-outboard, is a $75 optional for the outboard version.

Outboard powering has two pricing advantages over stern-drive propulsion. One lies in the nature of the power plants, the other is a matter of production. With an outboard, a single power unit is involved. With an inboard-outboard, there's what is called a power package—the engine as one unit and the stern drive as another, plus the hooking up of the two. The engine itself may cost more than an outboard motor of matching power. One reason is that most inboard engines operate on the four-cycle principle, same as your auto's engine, whereas most outboard motors are two-cycle. On the basis of performance, cost, and even weight per horsepower, the two-cycle outboard beats the inboard hands down. Moreover, the demand for outboards permits some approach to mass production, which means any savings in production is likely to be passed on to buyers. In comparison, marine inboard engines are produced in a relatively small way.

In some cases, however, because of production savings and lesser weight-per-horsepower of two-cycle engines, manufacturers power some of their stern units with inboards using the two-cycle principle. This gives them a price advantage. Moreover, the operational cost is likely to be alleviated by recent improvements designed to make two-cycle engines, both outboards and inboard-outboards, more economical in terms of fuel consumption and the gas-and-oil ratio required.

In trying to decide which type of buy, consider the amount of use you're likely to get from a bigger boat. Its extra roominess and comfort most likely will encourage you to make longer runs than you've been in the habit of making. The boat's greater seaworthiness may also open up new and larger waters to you. If this could be the case, it may be wise to shoulder the extra cost of the inboard-outboard, assuming you'll eventually make up the difference in fuel savings. Let's go back to those two boats we've been comparing.

At cruising speed, the large outboard will use, for example, 6 to 8 gallons of fuel an hour. The inboard-outboard's consumption should be half that or less. Making this difference more important will be the oil content of the outboard's fuel mix, which may increase the per-gallon or per-hour cost of operation appreciably. Generally, a $2 saving for each hour of running time is usual. In checking these figures with owners, one man with a two-year-old inboard-outboard claims he has already made up the extra $500 he spent in his original purchase. Another owner, though equally well satisfied with his boat, contends that he'd never catch up with the extra initial cost. Understandably, this difference of opinion arises from the fact that the first owner uses his inboard-outboard from early spring to late fall for fishing—about 150 hours per season. The other man's boat is used largely for afternoon cruising, about fifty hours of running time per season.

This same line of reasoning applies if you're considering an inboard-outboard with a small diesel engine rather than the conventional gasoline type. The diesel costs more to buy, but it consumes even less fuel, and the fuel itself is cheaper. If you use the boat enough, you'll eventually get back the extra initial cost.

While it is true that outboard-motor manufacturers have worked out engineering refinements that lessen fuel consumption and oil content necessary for proper lubrication, the healthy appetites of the large motors continues to put the outboard at a disadvantage in the popular 16 to 24-foot boat bracket.

How long are you likely to keep your boat? Whichever type you buy, and assuming the boat is satisfactory, are you likely to remain satisfied or are you one of those who prefer to trade in every year or so on something

Engine, uncovered here, is located in cockpit, making maintenance easy.

new and different? Large outboard rigs depreciate rather rapidly in trade-in value. Inboards, on the other hand, retain value better and longer. One of the advantages claimed for the inboard-outboards is that they compare favorably with the conventional inboard in this respect.

While it's debatable whether an inboard-type engine will outlast an outboard motor, a typical inboard-outboard installation has several features which could make the difference. For one thing, the engine is protected, not out in the open. That is an important consideration, especially in salt-water service. And, as commonly done for large inboards, the rig could be fitted with a fresh-water cooling system to safeguard the block and parts. Better maintenance is generally encouraged since the engine is conveniently located for servicing. So far as the stern-drive unit is concerned, that's largely up to the owner. Most drives can be lifted clear of the water, but few owners seem to do it, even when their boats are not being used for lengthy periods.

Except for the difference in weight, an inboard-outboard can be trail-ered as easily as an outboard. The inboard-outboard boat might weigh 1,250 pounds, and the outboard version 700 pounds plus around 200 pounds for the large motor.

While some inboard-outboard makers claim easy power-plant installa-tion, the comparison is with the inboard engine rather than the outboard motor. It's true that the large outboard motor with its accessories must be literally installed on the boat rather than merely mounted on the transom. The conventional inboard engine, however, is more costly to install and special skill is required to do the job right.

Here, again, the inboard-outboard's power package, as it is called, is a compromise between the two in being relatively easy to install. This is im-portant from two angles: 1. For the boat manufacturer, it's largely a matter of puncturing the transom and bolting the engine and drive units in place. 2. From the buyer's standpoint, the price tag is likely to include a minimum labor charge for installation.

14 Your New Power Plant

WHEN THE power plant is inboard, installation is handled by the boat-builder, and its initial servicing and a tune-up after the first twenty hours will likely be handled by the dealer. By carefully studying and faithfully following the recommendations in the owner's manual, the new owner can expect long and trouble-free performance.

The same might be said for outboard power. However, circumstances sometimes differ with the purchase of an outboard motor. Particularly with the smaller motors, there is a greater and natural tendency for the owner to assume the role of mechanic. Perhaps he recognizes a similarity with the two-cycle engine he has tinkered with on his lawn mower. Often an outboard motor is purchased separately. With the impatience of human nature, chances are he'll want to clamp it onto his boat and fire it up as soon as possible.

If you've just bought a new outboard motor, bear in mind that the performance and life of any fast-turning piece of machinery depend on how it's treated during the first few hours of use. If this is your first outboard, and you're going to "do it yourself," here are some suggestions:

There's likely to be a warranty card. Fill it out and either give it to your dealer or mail it to the factory, whichever is directed. In this way you register the warrant so that it will be in force if needed. Incidentally, don't knife that big carton apart in your anxiety. It's handy for storing the motor in the off-season.

With your motor you'll get an instruction manual; don't merely glance at it. It's packed full of valuable information. By studying it now, you'll gain valuable advance knowledge of your motor.

First, place the motor on a stand, or prop it securely against a wall. Remove its hood to expose the power head. Then take a comfortable seat alongside. As you read the manual, identify each motor part as it's mentioned. This way you get to know not only your motor but also the manual. In the future you'll be able to find quickly any needed information.

While you're at it, feel the electrical connections on the motor, and check exposed bolts and screws for tightness. When you read about care of the lower unit, remove its plug to see if the case is actually filled with lubricant. Motors are factory-checked on such points, but a slip-up can occur.

In your haste to see how the motor runs, don't make the mistake of trying it out in a barrel or tank. With the facilities an owner is likely to have, the water will get too warm to cool the motor effectively. Nor will an ordinary tank absorb the vibration of the running motor as well as will the transom of a water-borne boat; any prolonged running in such a tank will literally shake the motor to pieces.

In putting the motor on the boat, make it a habit to see that the clamp bracket is seated squarely on the transom. Don't use a wrench on the clamp screws, but turn them down evenly and as tightly as you can by hand. Have a safety wire or chain, even a temporary rope, tied from boat to motor to prevent losing the engine should it hop off the transom.

If the boat is a standard make, its transom height is probably right. However, you should adjust the angle of most motors carefully so that the drive shaft is straight up and down. Later you may find that this angle will change with different loads or speeds. You can reset the motor accordingly.

For starting, follow the step-by-step procedure recommended in your manual. First, though, you must have fuel in the tank. Right away you should become a crank about fuel. Unless yours is a Homelite outboard motor, it is two-cycle and depends on oil mixed in the fuel for its lubrication. An outboard motor that's fed improper fuel will run, but will suffer. More or less constant readjusting of the mixture controls may be required.

Check your instruction manual for the amount of oil recommended per gallon of gas. Don't add extra oil "just to be sure." That won't help the motor.

Use only outboard-motor oil. If its unavailable, use regular-grade automotive oil. The worst oils for two-cycle outboard motors are the high-priced "premium" or "heavy-duty" car oils. These may help to keep four-cycle car engines clean, but they have the opposite effect on a two-cycle outboard motor.

Gasolines with a high lead content and other additives can also be harmful to outboard motors. Marine white gas is the best grade to use; good-quality

Proper blend of fuel and oil will reduce chance of outboard breakdown. Always fill portable tanks on the dock, not in the boat, and strain the fuel.

regular gas is entirely satisfactory for any outboard engine used for pleasure.

Mixing a gallon or so of fuel for a small motor's daily requirements is an easy job, but mixing what a big motor uses definitely isn't. Worst of all, the more fuel involved, the less thorough the mixing is apt to be. Often a motor's misbehavior can be blamed on poor fuel mixing. And all the while the motor's life is being shortened by operating one minute on fuel with too much oil, and the next on practically raw gasoline.

A simple solution to this problem is to use ready-mixed outboard fuel. Naturally you should satisfy yourself about the reliability of the seller, but the requirements for such batch mixing are relatively simple. More and more waterside fuel docks and fishing camps, and even certain highway service stations, are providing ready-mixed fuel that is a better blend than the average owner mixes.

If you do the job yourself, here are some hints. In mixing for a small motor, use a container large enough to allow not only for the addition of oil but also for proper mixing. Rather than try to mix 5 gallons of fuel in a standard 5-gallon can, buy only 4 gallons of gas. Or for 1-gallon lots, have a 2-gallon can. Always pour in the gas (the lighter liquid) first, preferably half your amount. Then add the oil, and the rest of the gas. When it's all in, shake well.

Make it a practice to strain all fuel going into your tanks. Have a good-size funnel fitted with wire gauze or screening that's fine enough to catch water while allowing the fuel to pass through (a standard marine item). Then, as the stream of gasoline is fed into the funnel, dribble in your gas-thinned oil, trying to time this to last out the delivery of gas.

It's surprising what a wire screen will catch, especially in taking on gas at out-of-the-way places and stations with old pumps: lint, particles of trash, and frequently water. If you find more than the odd drops of water showing on the screen, take on only enough fuel to get safely to another fueling point.

Most new motors, except certain low-horsepower jobs, have a gearshift. An important advantage of this feature is that you can start the motor in neutral while you're tied to a dock, and remain there until you have it running smoothly. Avoid, however, any prolonged running of the motor in neutral. Nor should adjustments be made with the motor shifted to forward speed but the boat still tied to the dock. Only with the boat free to move can the motor operate at its best.

If the motor has no gearshift, paddle your boat well out from the shore and into a clear area. You want to be able to concentrate on starting and on keeping the motor going without worry of hitting obstructions or other boats.

Although there's no trick to starting an electric-starting model, a manual or rewind-starter motor requires a bit of getting onto. For one thing, your new motor is rather stiff to turn over. Start by getting the feel of the starter. Pull the cord out to where the pull gets increasingly hard. This is your signal that the engine is coming up on its compression (and firing) stroke. Return the starter handle to its original position. Then, after rechecking to see that you have the controls adjusted as directed for starting, brace yourself firmly, with one hand on the motor to keep it from tilting inward as you pull.

Pull the cord firmly but rapidly. Keep the handle in your hand until the cord has rewound itself; don't let it fly. You may have to make several tries before getting the engine to fire and start, but don't be discouraged. As you master the technique, and as the motor gradually frees up, you'll be more likely to make first-time starts.

Regardless of what anyone may tell you to the contrary, it's sensible to break in your motor gradually. After the motor is started, let it run at low speed for a couple of minutes—long enough to warm up. Then step the speed up tó half throttle, and run the motor that way for about twenty minutes. Then stop the motor and allow it to cool for several minutes.

Next you should run the motor at around two-thirds throttle for a total of five hours, which needn't be crowded into a single day. During this period, stop the motor occasionally to allow it to cool, spacing these cooling intervals farther apart as the motor wears in.

After the five-hour period of initial breaking in, you can safely rev the motor up to full power. But do it for short periods only, not yet continuously. Adjust the high-speed control to give the smoothest running.

It's wise at this stage of the break-in to change the lubricant in the lower unit. Sometimes the oil seal will be slow in seating, allowing water to get in. Or the lubricant may have picked up some steel dust as the fine tool marks on the gear teeth are worn smooth.

Make it a habit to check the discharge of cooling water after starting the motor. In shallow-water operation, continue to check it occasionally. Also keep the propeller clear of weeds. Always carry a spare set of clean and properly adjusted spark plugs.

It's a good idea to change the speed of the motor every so often even after breaking it in. This helps keep down carbon deposits.

If the boat is kept at home on a trailer and is used infrequently, say only weekends, the motor should be flushed out with fresh water after each trip. Most owners use a garden hose, washing salt deposits off the boat and trailer at the same time. Some motors have a flushing nozzle, otherwise you can buy a clip-on device for the job. In either case, don't use full city-water pressure. The motor's pump, designed to draw water in, may be damaged if full force is used.

If the boat is used frequently and kept in the water or at a dock, the motor is not likely to be flushed periodically. Such treatment, however, doesn't seem to harm the modern motor. There are even two schools of thought as to whether the lower unit should be left in the water or raised out. One group claims that air cannot get into the cooling system of a submerged unit and, therefore, corrosion cannot take place. The other group holds that air can get in through the exhaust ports and that, in any case, barnacles can get a good start on a submerged unit, possibly restricting the water intake. But all agree that motors should be flushed thoroughly prior to winter storage.

Another precaution is to check the grease in the lower unit as often as necessary to have it always completely packed. It's also wise to grease the motor's swivel pin, on which the motor turns for steering, and the exterior linkage of the control system.

A motor carried in a car trunk should be cushioned in some way, and blocked against bumping about. One way is to nest it in a partially inflated old inner tube.

Don't rest a motor on a sandy beach for any length of time without covering it. Wind-blown sand can find its way into the carburetor, and possibly into the cylinders, by way of the exhaust system.

If you stand the motor against a tree or your car, fasten it somehow so that it can't fall over to damage controls or other parts.

To tilt the motor when it's on the boat, reach behind the cowl and pull up; don't tilt it by pushing down on the steering handle.

The following is a list of the possible causes of the more common outboard motor troubles together with suggestions for correcting them.

MOTOR WILL NOT START

Fuel Valve or vent closed.
Open it.

Tank empty.
Fill with correct fuel mixture.

Carburetor float-valve stuck.
Fuel will drip from carburetor. Tap lightly to free float.

Fouled or defective spark plugs.
Remove them and install spare set, or carefully clean old ones.

Crankcase flooded.
Remove spark plugs and examine for dampness (oil or fuel). If wet, wipe clean. Meanwhile, crank motor several times with plugs out. Put plugs back in, making sure to include gasket. Then try cranking motor again.

Fuel line clogged.
Depress carburetor float pin. Fuel should drip from carburetor. If fuel does not flow, disconnect fuel pipe and remove any obstruction. If fuel pipe is not at fault, clean fuel strainer. For a pressurized system, check line for kinks or damage, condition of bulb, and tightness of metal ferules and connections.

Magneto points fouled or out of adjustment, or ignition system generally defective.
Check by removing one plug, holding it by rubber boot, and ground it against block where you can watch gap while turning engine over. If a good spark shows, magneto is O.K. If not,

and plug is in good condition, clean and adjust or replace breaker points. Better still, have a reputable repair man check it.

Battery starting. Poor or no response.
Weak or dead battery. Check terminals for tightness and clean off any corrosion. Check tightness of nuts holding wires at junction box.

Stop switch shorted.
Inspect switch and its wiring.

MOTOR STARTS & STOPS

Fuel tank air vent not open or clogged.
Open, making sure it is clean.

Out of fuel.
Tank empty, or a pressurized system may not be feeding properly.

Fuel passages obstructed.
Motor will run for a while and stop. Clean fuel pipes and filter. If carburetor is clogged, take motor to an outboard service station.

Loose or defective wiring.
Inspect all wires for cracked or badly chafed insulation. If necessary, wipe clean and expose to sun until dry. Tape any breaks and make all connections tight.

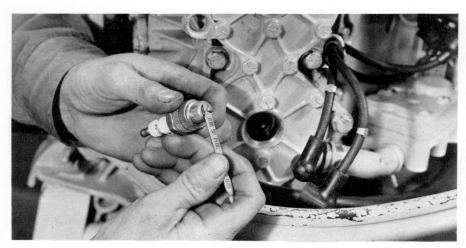

Check spark-plug gap. It's especially important in two-cycle engines.

MOTOR MISSES

Spark plugs fouled.
Remove. Replace or clean.

Plugs wrong heat range or gap wrong.
Replace with proper spark plug with gap as specified in motor's maintenance booklet.

Incorrect fuel adjustment.
Carburetor needs readjusting. First, be sure that your fuel mix is correct and thoroughly mixed.

Dirt or water in fuel.
Drain small quantity into a container and check for dirt or water. If present, drain and flush tank and refill with clean fuel.

Loose or defective wiring.
Check for faulty insulation, connections.

Magneto trouble.
Check for spark.

Air leak in intake manifold or connection.
Listen for indication of leakage while cranking motor. Tightening bolts or screws may correct condition, but when possible have a mechanic check it.

MOTOR KNOCKS

Fuel mixture too rich.
Try with fresh, properly mixed fuel. If condition persists, have carburetor checked.

Loose flywheel.
Take up on flywheel nut.

Excessive carbon in cylinders.
Motor needs overhauling and cleaning.

MOTOR SUDDENLY RACES

Shear pin broken.
Stop motor immediately. Remove propeller and propeller nut and replace shear pin. Replace propeller and tighten nut.

MOTOR OVERHEATS

Fuel mix wrong.
Check booklet to be sure you're using correct portion of oil and mix with fuel thoroughly.

Insufficient cooling water.
Check intake for obstructions, then the water passages. In an old motor, latter may need shop attention.

Motor not deep enough in water.
Lowering indicated. But consult mechanic before cutting down boat's transom notch.

MOTOR SUDDENLY STOPS

Out of fuel.
Check tank. See if vent is open. Make sure it isn't plugged.

Fuel mix wrong.
Too little oil, or poorly mixed.

Insufficient lubricant in lower unit.
Refill according to directions. Motor may loosen up after cooling off. Squirting a little oil in cylinders should help. Don't use too much force in attempting to turn motor over. Determine true cause if this condition continues.

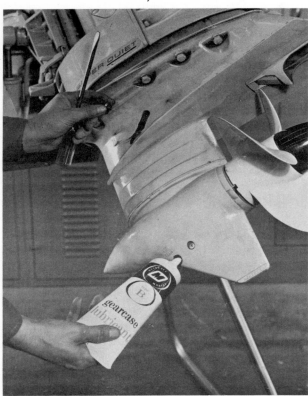

Force lubricant in lower hole until it shows at top hole.

NO POWER UNDER HEAVY LOAD

Carburetor adjustments off.
Mixture lean, or too rich. Have carburetor checked.

Insufficient fuel.
Check tank vent, fuel lines, or filter for obstructions. Pump or pressurized system may be starving carburetor.

Weeds or other debris in propeller or lower unit.
Check and clear.

Wrong propeller.
If your service is unusual, check with your dealer to see if a special propeller would help.

GENERATOR WON'T CHARGE

Battery condition.
Defective or weak. Possibly dirty or loose connections. For an A.C. generator, check fuse.

15 Trailers

IF THE BOAT you own or contemplate acquiring is of a trailerable size, a good trailer will add a new dimension to your boating. In addition to expanding your range, it will keep down the cost of boat maintenance. This is particularly true as one steps up to larger boats. By keeping a boat on a trailer in the backyard or driveway, or still better under a carport, you avoid charges for summer dockage and winter storage. You can more easily keep your boat clean and free from bottom fouling. And ordinarily, you reduce the possibilities of vandalism and damage by passing craft.

The most attractive advantage, however, is that your cruising and fishing waters can be just as far away as you want to drive, and the trailered boat increases the amount of gear you can take along.

Make sure, however, that the trailer suits the boat. Just any trailer won't do—and they are not interchangeable. A modern trailer designed for your particular type boat should usually load and unload without dunking the wheel bearings. Tilting beds and power winches will ease the job of loading and unloading without the need for getting even your feet wet.

Fishing service particularly is notoriously hard on trailers. Most of us carry more gear in our loaded boats than the average pleasure-boat owner. We drive the backroads more, often launching wherever it's possible to reach the water. Therefore, select your trailer with care and then give it the care it deserves. The surest way of avoiding trouble on the road, and in launching or loading, is to select a well-built trailer designed to take a craft the next size larger than your boat.

A trailer properly set up to carry your boat will have support directly under the transom when the stem is snug against the bow stop. Weight will be centered over supports—with an inboard, this means under engine stringers.

Load your boat with a plan, so that the first items needed are easy to get to. And this might include the icebox and cooking equipment for a quick meal along the roadside or on reaching your destination. Protect bedding and clothing with waterproof cover or your tent in case of rain. Air mattresses, partially inflated will give good padding for breakables. Use shock cord to lash down loose gear.

Don't take chances on overloading your trailer. Check with the manufacturer on the maximum capacity of your trailer and don't exceed it. If

The expense of docking and mooring are eliminated and costly maintenance reduced by using a trailer.

With your boat on a trailer, you can do your boating on any waters that you can reach by car. Also, a trailer allows you to carry more gear.

you do, you can expect failure of bearings, tires or damage to the trailer frame and possible damage to your boat. The load you are carrying may surprise you. If you can locate a drive-on scale (at your local railroad station, lumber yard, or coal yard) check the weight of your trailer when loaded with boat, motor, luggage, camping equipment, fishing tackle, fuel and other gear normally carried.

When a modern trailer sways, it is apt to be caused by improper loading. The load should be slightly tongue-heavy—about 5 percent of the total weight for rigs up to 1500 pounds. Over 1500 pounds, the tongue should be about 7 percent heavier and your car should be equipped with an equalizing hitch connected to the automobile frame—not the bumper. You can sometimes adjust the balance sufficiently by merely shifting the heavy movable items carried in the boat. But be sure that the heavy items are centered over cradle support.

If you've made changes in your rig, such as a new motor or the addition of a spare fuel tank to the trailer, check to see if the unit needs rebalancing.

Largely through the efforts of industry-sponsored legislation campaigns, state laws are gradually becoming more uniform. But, there are some variations. A digest of the boat trailer laws is available from the Outboard Boating Club of America, 333 N. Michigan Ave., Chicago, Illinois. If you plan to travel across state lines, you would do well to send for a copy and study it. By making your rig conform with the most rigid laws, you can travel with confidence.

Watch the speed limits. Often they are lower when pulling a trailer, and some throughways and parkways restrict them to certain hours or prohibit them entirely. Don't forget license and registration for the trailer. Also, check on your insurance, particularly for trailering.

Follow the manufacturer's recommendations for tire pressure and check them frequently—they'll wear longer.

Heavier loads, 4,000 pounds and more, require tandem wheels on the trailer. When you get into the larger trailers especially, consider the practicality of mounting tires and wheels of the same size as your car so that they are interchangeable in an emergency. In any case, be sure you carry a spare tire mounted on a spare wheel for the trailer and be sure you also have a jack which will work on the trailer. Your automobile jack won't work unless it is of the type that slides under the axle—a bumper jack won't help.

Learn to drive smoothly when trailering: accelerate slowly and brake slowly. Check your mirrors constantly, giving your rig plenty of room and other traffic a wide berth. Keep at least a 300-foot distance from the car in front of you and make no sudden moves without signalling your intention.

Don't overwork your brakes. Use a pumping action to slow your momentum and when descending a hill use a lower gear or your engine's compression to keep control. Practice backing on a deserted parking lot. You'll find there is a bit of delay between the time you turn the steering wheel and the trailer begins to respond. Keep your eye on the rear end of the rig and guide it around slowly, avoiding the disastrous jackknife. It won't take long to get the feeling without having to studiously remind yourself to turn in the direction opposite your intended direction.

On long trips, be sure to carry road flares or emergency warning lights.

Don't neglect your trailer. Inspect all parts for signs of weakness.

Clean and oil the coupler and winch regularly. Check the winch cable and safety chain, replacing them when they show wear. Check lighting harness and lights. Remove rust spots as they appear and replace bulbs that have burned out or ones with broken filaments. Clean and oil all moving parts on the tilting mechanism and rollers. Check rollers and cradle pads, replacing any that show signs of wear. Any unusual gouges or worn spots may indicate poor alignment and the need for repositioning them under the boat.

We'd suggest that you have the dealer or a competent garage mechanic check your wheel bearings. Every time you stop at a service station, check the temperature of the wheel hubs with your hand. If they are unduly hot, have them serviced at once.

Periodically inspect the frame, tongue, fenders, and winch mast for rust spots. Rub such spots down to bare metal with emery paper and retouch with matching color paint. Touch up and repaint your trailer as needed, but don't paint over rust—clean rusty spots and prime them before painting.

Never risk questionable tires or a weak hitch—replace them.

If you put up your trailer for the winter, block up the tongue to keep it out of the mud. Jack up the axle and set it on blocks to take the weight off the tires. The tires will last longer if the wheels and tires are stored inside where they are cool and dry. Clean the winch carefully; in fact you'll prolong its useful life if you would remove it and store it in a dry place in the house or garage. While you're at it, carefully inspect the cable. At the first signs of fraying, you might turn it end for end and use it another season. If it's worn to the point of weakness, of course replace it.

16 How To Pass Inspection

IN RECENT YEARS the authorities charged with enforcement of boating laws and regulations—federal, state, and county—have been tightening up on boat owners. This increasing law enforcement usually takes the form of boat inspections, mainly spot checks to see if the required safety equipment is aboard and up to required standards.

For example, the U.S. Coast Guard has put a number of mobile units into operation, with particular concentration in areas of peak boating activity.

These boarding units consist of men specially trained to inspect small boats and call their shortcomings to the attention of the owners. Team equipment includes a 16-foot outboard, and a truck and trailer. Teams spend a week at each site checking boats both in the water and as launched. Boarding-unit members have the power of arrest, but Coast Guard officials say this is rarely used. Part of the work of these unit members is to teach state officials how to do the job.

The Coast Guard's Recreational Boating Safety Division has revealed that during the 1965 season 58 percent of the craft boarded were in violation. While 43.8 percent of these merely violated numbering and registration regulations, another 34.7 percent failed to heed safety rules. This latter figure included 20.7 percent with improper or insufficient life preservers and 14 per-

A U. S. Coast Guard mobile team boards 30-foot cabin cruiser for spot inspection.

Marine police of Richmond, California, on daily patrol in local harbor waters.

cent without proper fire extinguishers. Inadequate ventilation accounted for 10 percent of the infractions and a multitude of miscellaneous categories made up the balance.

Then there is the Coast Guard Auxiliary, a civilian body which works somewhat in conjunction with the Coast Guard but without the latter's authority. An important part of its work is to conduct what are called courtesy examinations of boats and equipment. The auxiliary reports that better than half of the boats examined by their members fail to pass the safety requirements.

The Coast Guard Auxiliary operates pretty much throughout the country and many of their members are qualified vessel examiners. To locate the operating unit in your area, write to the U.S. Coast Guard Auxiliary, National Headquarters, Washington 25, D.C.

Their qualified members examine, rather than inspect . . . you volunteer to have your boat and its equipment examined. There is no obligation, nor is there any fee involved. Their examiners offer advice as well as checking equipment. If an examination reveals a certain item as being unacceptable,

Coast Guard Auxiliary officers inspect gear for rule violations.

Courtesy examination decal is awarded if boat is properly equipped.

you'll be told why and advised how to go about replacing it. Also, in such a case, the examination will not be stopped there. Instead, the examiner will complete his entire check and discuss with you, as one boat owner to another, how to correct other shortcomings found. He will also be familiar with your state's safety requirements. If your boat fails this first examination, its deficiencies will not be reported to any enforcement authorities, nor will a record be kept of them. Moreover, you'll be advised that the auxiliary will gladly reexamine your boat upon request, after you've corrected the deficiencies.

The U.S. Coast Guard is charged with enforcement of federal laws upon the navigable waters of the United States and its possessions, and on the high seas. Since most of the enforcement work is preventive and educational, the Coast Guard, by its own definition more nearly resembles a national Department of Public Safety than an ordinary police force.

The Motorboat Act of 1940 and the Federal Boating Act of 1958, with amendments, are designed primarily to protect inexperienced or careless boatmen.

By law, each of the three classes of pleasure boats up to 65 feet long must be equipped with specified lights, sound-signal equipment, lifesaving equipment, fire extinguishers and ventilation. Registration is required for powerboats of more than 10 h.p., boarding for inspection is authorized, and any boat operator may be required to show identification.

The Rules of the Road, which deal with lights, fog signals, speed, steering, right of way, operations in narrow channels, and distress signals, are actually four sets of rules: International (high seas), Inland (rivers and harbors), Western Rivers, and Great Lakes. These differ considerably, making uniform enforcement impossible. But, the ponderous lawmaking machinery is inching toward bringing them all into harmony. The boating trades' organizations, with Coast Guard encouragement, have a continuing program to promote uniform state boating laws as well as approved standards for the manufacture of safe equipment.

LIGHTS

If you are going to use your boat at night, you need running lights to satisfy the Coast Guard. Rowing boats must have ready at hand a lantern showing a white light which shall be temporarily exhibited in sufficient time to prevent collision.

If your boat is under 26 foot long and you use it only on inland waters, western rivers, and the Great Lakes, you must have a combination red-and-green light on the bow and a white stern light. The bow light must show red to port and green to starboard from dead ahead to two points abaft (astern of) the beam, and must be visible for one mile. The white stern light must be visible for two miles all around the horizon.

Proper placement of the bow light on small boats can be troublesome. When the construction of the boat dictates that it be placed some distance from the extreme forward point of the bow, be sure it is mounted high enough to be visible if your boat rides bow high.

Boats from 26 foot to 65 foot in length must have a red port side light and a green starboard side light, each screened to be visible for a mile from right ahead to two points abaft the beam. The bow light is white and must be visible for two miles from right ahead to two points abaft the beam. The stern light is white and visible for two miles over the entire horizon.

International Rules require a somewhat different arrangement of lights, but these rules apply to boats used on the high seas.

SOUND-SIGNAL EQUIPMENT

All powerboats (including outboards) over 16 feet long must carry a whistle "or other sound-producing mechanical appliance" to prevent collision in crossing and passing situations, and for giving signals in fog. Class 1 craft (from 16 feet to 26 feet) can carry a lung-powered whistle audible a half mile. On Class 2 boats (26 feet to 40 feet) it must be audible a mile away, which means the whistle must operate by hand or power. On Class 3 boats (40 feet to 65 feet) it must be an electric or air-powered device with a range of one mile.

SIGNALS IN FOG:
    Underway — 1 long blast every minute
    At anchor — ring bell rapidly for five seconds every minute
SIGNALS IN CLEAR WEATHER:
    Underway — 1 long blast when backing from dock
    1 short blast signifies that you are directing your course to starboard
    2 short blasts signify that you are directing your course to port
    3 short blasts signify that your engines are going full speed astern
    4 short blasts signify danger. They can also signify

doubt or disagreement with the signaled intention of an approaching boat.

LIFESAVING EQUIPMENT

All boats of less than 40 feet in length are required to carry one Coast Guard approved life preserver, buoyant vest, ring buoy, or buoyant cushion in serviceable condition for each person on board. Keep these stored in some easily accessible place, and where the air can get to them. Be certain that all safety equipment purchased for your boat bears a tag giving details of approval and instructions for use, and don't remove those tags. As a jacket or cushion gets old, check its condition—don't take chances with worn-out equipment. If you have any doubts about approval of the type of equipment you have or are considering, write to the U.S. Coast Guard for a copy of their free *Equipment List CG-190*.

The Coast Guard specifies that life preservers be colored with International Orange; we recommend that all lifesaving gear be so colored—if you have to use the equipment, you want to be sure to be seen.

Outboard boats under 26 feet, if they are of open construction and not carrying passengers for hire, are not required to carry fire extinguishers. There is so much confusion about the meaning of the term "open construction" and such a questionable saving in the exemption, that we feel all gasoline-powered boats should conform to the minimum requirements listed below.

Fire extinguishers are classified by the types of fires they combat and by the size of the extinguisher. Class A extinguishers are for fires of ordinary combustible materials; Class B for flammable liquids and greases; Class C for electrical fires.

Powerboats under 26 feet in length must have at least one B-1 type extinguisher. A B-1 type can be either a 2-pound dry chemical, a 4-pound carbon dioxide, or a 1¼-gallon foam extinguisher.

Powerboats from 26 feet to 40 feet long must have at least two extinguishers of this type.

Powerboats from 40 feet to 65 feet in length must carry three such extinguishers. Regulations permit the substitution of one B-11 extinguisher for two B-1's. The larger B-11 contains either 10 pounds of dry chemical, 15 pounds of carbon dioxide, or 2½ gallons of foam. Have your extinguishers checked periodically by your dealer to be sure they are always rated in top condition.

VENTILATION

Coast Guard regulations require that "there shall be at least one exhaust duct installed so as to extend from the open atmosphere to the lower portion of the bilge and at least one intake duct installed so as to extend to a point at least midway to the bilge or at least below the level of the carburetor air intake."

The ventilator cowls "shall be located and trimmed for maximum effectiveness and in such a manner as to prevent displaced fumes from being recirculated."

Only open boats do not require ventilating cowls and ducts. These, the regulations say, are "motorboats or motor vessels with all engine and fuel tank compartments, and other spaces to which explosive or flammable gases and vapors from these compartments may flow, open to the atmosphere and so arranged as to prevent the entrapment of such gases and vapors within the vessel."

All other craft must comply, and this includes inboards, stern-drives, auxiliaries, and many outboard-powered boats.

All models of stock boats from 1966 on are almost certain to comply, and older models may not, and will have to be altered to conform in order to pass inspection. The Coast Guard set June 1, 1967 as the date for total compliance. If you are in doubt about a particular installation, the following publications spell out the requirements: *Engineering Manual of Recommended Practices,* issued by the Boating Industry Association, 307 N. Michigan Ave., Chicago, Ill. 60601; and *Fire Protection Standard for Motor Craft,* published by the National Fire Protection Association, 60 Batterymarch St., Boston, Mass. 02109.

YOU WILL ALSO NEED

What might be classed as operating equipment usually isn't legally required. Still, any experienced owner regards certain items as necessary for the well-being of his boat and the safety of those aboard. Some state acts require an anchor and line, and the Coast Guard Auxiliary in its recommendations for additional equipment lists both items as essential for even Class A boats. Other items on this list are oars or paddle, a pump or bailer, and flares.

For other than very small outboards, the anchor should be some standard type. To insure holding, its weight must be in keeping with the size and type of the boat. Also, the length of the line must allow what is known as scope. That is, it must be long enough to angle back to the boat, where the craft will be held some distance away from the anchor by wind or current. A line seven times the depth is not too much. Naturally, the line must also be strong enough to withstand the strain. Your marine supply store will have manufacturers' tables listing anchor weights and rope sizes suitable for different types and lengths of boats. It's wise to buy in the upper bracket of what's recommended for your boat.

If the craft is to be used on strange waters where you'll occasionally be out of sight of land, charts and a proper compass are essential items. Also, it often helps to know the depth of water. You can determine this by hand sounding, but it can be done much more conveniently with an electronic sounder.

Next are those items which are being considered emergency equipment. Small boats should have at least a bailer; larger ones an actual bilge pump.

It's a good idea to carry distress flares aboard any boat used on open waters. You should also have a first-aid kit, a small kit of engine tools, and certain spare motor parts. The minimum requirements for a small outboard are a screwdriver, pliers, and adjustable wrench, and possibly a spark-plug wrench. Spare parts should include a set of clean, dry spark plugs, and shear pins, if they are used. Include a roll of friction tape, lubricating oil, a tube of grease, and a small can of carbon tetrachloride for cleaning oil or water-fouled plugs. And don't forget your motor's instruction manual.

Set this as your standard: Equip your boat so that you can operate and sustain yourself and crew through any condition that might arise in your type of boating activities. Then, in case of inspection, your rig should pass any requirements. More important, you'll be insuring your own safety afloat.

17 Lowdown on Boat Insurance

MARINE INSURANCE is a highly complicated subject and judging from our discussions with people who make their living in the insurance business, it requires a specialist's full time to keep informed. One expert pointed out the fact that today's basic marine insurance policies still bear a resemblance to the contracts written before the time of Columbus. That today's small-boat operator has little else in common with Columbus might give us cause for some concern.

For this reason, the first thing to do when you're considering insurance is to choose an agent who has a reputation for thorough knowledge of the marine aspects of the business. Tell him what you have in mind, and have him tell you what coverage he would recommend.

So you will have some ammunition for your discussion, let's see if we can define the basic needs and the common methods of handling them.

But, you may say, you don't need insurance. Your outfit didn't cost much, you use it on quiet waters, and you've become a fairly capable boatman. That may be true, but it's well to realize that boating today is no longer the simple sport it used to be. Though an outstanding job is being done keeping boating's accident rate low, there's been a widespread increase in accidents and incidents of a sort which don't make the headlines or get into the records but which are troublesome and costly for those involved.

Even if yours is the most modest rig, you can still be held liable for injury to or death of others, and for damage to property of others. You can purchase insurance to protect yourself against this liability. There is no ceiling on the amount of damages that may be awarded against you for your negligence in the operation of your boat. It is therefore important that you protect yourself adequately.

You can cover your liability for bodily injury and property damage with an all-risk policy on your boat; under a comprehensive personal liability or family liability policy; or as part of your homeowner's policy. Inboards of more than 50 h.p. and outboards of more than 25 h.p. require an additional premium when added to the last two policies.

You may feel obliged to pay the medical expenses of guests injured on your boat even when you are not legally liable. You can cover yourself for these costs through the same policies listed in the paragraph above.

Rarely are yards held responsible for accidents involving use of their gear.

So far, the insurance mentioned is only that which reimburses the other fellow, and we'll return to this later. But, what about protecting your own investment—boat, motor, trailer, accessories—against fire, theft, collision, sinking and stranding?

Unfortunately, theft and vandalism have become so prevalent that few marinas will assume responsibility for such losses. At places which feature 24-hour watchman service, rates are usually so high that carrying insurance is the cheaper way of securing protection.

The situation can be almost as bad when one keeps his boat on a trailer in his own yard or driveway. It's not unusual for such rigs to be hauled away in their owner's absence, and, if recovered, valuable equipment is likely to be missing.

Fast outboards need insurance protection against growing collision rate.

124

Fire often results in total loss of boats.

Expensive equipment left aboard a boat at its slip is a standing invitation to thieves. Most stolen gear is the type that's inconvenient or impractical to carry back and forth, and locks are no real safeguard.

Let's try to summarize some of the different insurance coverages or policies now available to boat owners, remembering that each may be offered with variations to suit special circumstances.

Limited-Named Perils Insurance This form of policy provides coverage for certain specific perils, such as fire and lightning, collision, derailment, or overturning of a transporting land conveyance, windstorm on land, and

Care at fuel dock prevents fires, but owner should be protected.

theft. To recover damages under such a policy, the loss suffered must be caused by one of the named perils.

Broad-Named Perils. This type of policy in general provides somewhat broader coverage against additional named perils, such as collision with another vessel or object while afloat, perils of the sea, and loss of the motor overboard.

All-Risk or Comprehensive Insurance. The distinguishing feature about this form of policy is the insuring clause. Instead of listing the perils by name, the policy simply states that it protects the insured property against "all risks of physical loss or damage except as excluded." Often there is a deductible clause which provides that the insured bear a portion of the loss. This may range in amount from about $25 to $100.

The exclusions are explained as being items beyond normal control, or use of the equipment for commercial purposes, or for purposes which involve immoral or illegal acts. Many of the exclusions involve situations that the average owner is not likely to encounter, but there are some that he could run into. These include use of the boat in an official race or speed test, its use as a public livery or in situations where the equipment is rented to others, wear, tear, and depreciation or latent defects, fishing tackle, cameras and other personal effects not connected with boating.

These policies may or may not contain a lay-up clause. Outboard policies are usually more liberal, but inboard policies generally limit the actual in-the-water use of the boat to the accepted length of the boating season. For example, some policies state that the boat must be laid up or stored by October for the insurance to stay in effect. Most companies, however, will extend the season upon request. For year-around use, they may charge on additional premium.

Some companies issuing these policies may restrict the insurance coverage to specific sections of the country, others may not. Hence, it would be a good idea for boatmen who do extensive cruising to make sure in advance that the insurance they intend to buy would be in force wherever they go.

While all-risk policies are the most popular, they are also the most expensive. However, compared with rates for inboard-powered craft, outboard insurance is cheap. About 4 percent of the value of the boat and motor is a typical premium. Some companies charge a lower rate for the trailer. And with most companies, the cost is lower if you buy insurance for two or three years instead of one.

Rates vary geographically, tending to be slightly higher in the South, because of the longer season, and lower in the North. They also vary with density of population and with the degree of boating activity in one section as against another. Rates applying to boats kept and used in and around New York City, for example, are considerably higher than those applying to craft kept and used on remote lakes and rivers.

It's well to remember that this is a highly competitive field, and that when a rate seems particularly attractive there is likely to be a reason for it. For instance, some policies do not provide coverage when the boat is overloaded or overpowered. And those are factors not easily determined. Actually, any policy is likely to have provisions that could be construed one way or the other, in your favor or not, depending largely on the attitude of the local agent or representative who makes the survey.

The deductible clause is a good feature since it permits the company to offer lower rates and works no great hardship on the owner. Incidentally, the deductible usually applies only to the owner's own equipment. Any loss payable to another because of damage or injury from the action of the insured equipment usually is paid in full.

A good all-risk policy should provide protection for boat, motor, equipment, accessories, and a trailer specifically designed for transporting boats. There should also be an additional provision for property damage liability (damage you may do another boat, for instance). Liability coverage is usually $500, but some companies set the limit at $1,000. And one boat plan is unique in that it provides a sliding scale based on the amount of the policy. For example, with a $2,000 policy you'd have liability protection up to that amount.

Liability Coverage. Boating accidents may not only cause damage to property but may also injure persons—passengers, swimmers, for example. Ensuing lawsuits may result in large awards being made to the injured parties. Even if the boat owner is acquitted of responsibility, legal costs could be high. Liability coverage—insurance that protects you against such misfortunes, may be purchased in several ways as follows:

Protection and Indemnity. This is a type of marine insurance usually applied to inboard boats, and it is generally obtainable only as part of a fire or all-risks plan. An outboard owner may be able to get it in this form. It is expensive.

Comprehensive Personal Liability. You may already have such coverage or its equivalent if you have homeowner's insurance. This protects you against all accidents resulting from your activities wherever you may be, including the operation of your boat. Some plans even cover medical payments. However, read your policy to see what it says about outboard motor horsepower. If your motor is in excess of a certain horsepower, usually 25, an endorsement may be required and an extra premium may be charged.

If this extra cost is excessive, check with your outboard insurance agent. Maybe he can give you the same protection at a lower cost under your marine policy.

In any case, the premium will also be set by the amount of protection bought. Understandably, this is big-amount insurance, as warranted by the risks. The amount or limit that you can carry varies from a minimum, usually $10,000, up to $300,000.

Some companies offer a lower rate on their all-risk policy if the operator of the boat is over 21 years old. In the inboard field, some companies screen applicants carefully, taking only those considered to be preferred risks. This, combined with a rather high deductible clause, permits lower rates. With outboard rigs becoming bigger and more costly, this system could eventually be applied to the outboard field. Incidentally, insurance companies classify inboard-outboard boats as inboards.

Accessories. Another insurance problem resulting from the increased use of electronic equipment is getting a policy that is definite on the point of equipment. Suppose an owner installed an expensive accessory on his boat after his policy was issued. Would it be covered? What about portable radios and other gear borrowed from home for use aboard a boat? Some companies describe the type of accessories they will cover, while others cover them without definition. In any case, if you have expensive equipment aboard, such as a depth sounder, portable radio, and ship-to-shore phone, check with your agent to see if your policy covers such equipment. If the gear isn't covered, he may have a policy that will take it in.

Finance Plan Insurance. Many have been deceived by this type of policy. Insurance included in a finance plan for a boat seldom protects the owner adequately. Issued usually by the loan agency, it protects its interest in the outfit. You could be left out in the cold should something unfortunate happen. Again, check with your agent and get whatever additional protection you need.

Depreciation. As a rule, motors depreciate faster than boats, and some boats will depreciate faster than others. In case of loss, your insurance company will pay the actual cash value "with proper deduction for depreciation not exceeding the cost to repair or replace with materials of like kind and quality." For example, if you paid $1,200 for your boat six years ago, it may not be worth more than $500 today. Hence, why carry insurance for $1,200 year after year? Some companies handle this by taking depreciation into account and reducing the amount of the policy and premium each year.

On the contrary, if you don't carry sufficient insurance, you're likely to encounter what's called a co-insurer's clause, which means you become a co-insurer and share a certain percentage of any loss incurred. A friend's boat was worth a good $800, but he insured it for only $400. The boat suffered damages estimated at $200. But because of his policy's 100 percent co-insurance clause, he was only able to collect $100.

Cancelling. At first, it may seem economical to cancel your insurance at the end of the boating season. However, there is usually a minimum charge for a policy and you may not save much. If your policy is an all-risks type, you might as well continue to enjoy its broad coverage throughout the winter. You should continue this protection if you store your boat in someone's care. Covered storage sheds and even crowded outside storage areas are frequently firetraps where boats are worked on during the winter and spring months.

You'd think that a boat would be safe enough if stored in its owner's yard, driveway, or elsewhere on his premises, but that isn't always so. One insurance agent told us that among claims his company paid last year was one for $2,100 on a boat-and-trailer rig that disappeared from its owner's driveway. Apparently, someone just backed into the drive, knocked the supporting blocks clear of the trailer, and drove off with the works. A classic case concerned an owner who stored his boat in his garage. About the time he was ready to move it out, his wife sideswiped it while parking the family car. The insurance company paid in full.

18   Small-Boat Handling

WHEN YOU first take the helm of a boat, you're going to have to forget most of what you learned about driving an automobile.

With a boat, steering as well as power is exerted at the rear. When the propeller turns, it discharges a stream of water and the stern of the boat reacts by moving in a direction opposite to the discharge. Steering then, is accomplished by changing the direction of the discharge. With outboard and stern-drive power, the entire lower unit is turned to change the direction of the boat. With an inboard engine, the shaft is fixed and steering is accomplished by deflecting the discharge with a rudder.

With outboard and stern-drive power, action and reaction is positive and boats so powered are more maneuverable than a single-engine inboard boat. This becomes even more noticeable when reversing. Here again, when you can turn the entire lower unit, you have positive action and reaction. But when reversing with an inboard the rudder has no influence on the discharge and therefore loses its effectiveness. Boats with twin inboard engines gain maneuverability when the direction of one engine is put into opposition with the other, thereby twisting the boat around.

Another factor you'll have to cope with is the matter of braking—which, of course, is managed by reversing the power and the discharge of water.

Study the effect of your motor's propeller thrust at various speeds and angles on your boat's movements. While you're at it, notice how the wind affects what you're attempting. Also check or visualize the effect of any current or tide.

THE ART OF HELMSMANSHIP

It is important to know your boat's stopping distance at various speeds. Pick out a stationary object and shove back the throttle to check the distance required to reach a slow speed. Then, using neutral and reverse, find out how long it takes to bring the boat to a dead stop. Practice turning off the stationary object to note how far the stern skids at various speeds. Finally, try putting your boat right alongside the marker, stopping it dead there, as if you were going to dock. Use caution in your approaching and stopping at first, but gradually learn to do this in a more dashing way. If there's a strong wind blowing, or a fast current, make your approaches from different directions to note the varying effects.

Often conditions prevent you from making a slow, cautious approach. Suppose the wind is strong, or the tide is running swiftly. The area off the dock is crowded, and the dock itself is pretty much occupied except for the short space alongside the fuel pumps, meaning that you can't get lined-up properly for your approach. It's under such adverse conditions that an experienced boatman can give an outstanding exhibition of handling. He'll bring his boat through the fleet, turn sharply just to leeward of the dock and maintain speed until almost upon it. Then, at the last moment, by spinning his wheel and backing down fast, he'll swing the stern parallel to the dock, putting the boat about 6 inches off it.

There is seldom a need to expose yourself to such tough conditions during your learning period. Try to pick your times and places. If the dock is crowded, wait until enough boats have pulled away to leave you a reasonable length of open space to enter. Approach against the tide, or a strong wind, never with either on your stern, if you can avoid it. This way the current or wind tends to brake your speed. In the final stages, you can hold the boat in position or nudge it ahead slowly. Your aim should be to get the boat's bow off the spot where you want to dock, and with the stern not too far out. Next, by spinning the wheel and using a short burst of speed, the push of the prop will shove the stern in.

For some situations, it's wise to put your boat well beyond the slot you're aiming at, and then back in, finishing up by using a quick burst of speed in forward to straighten the boat or better your position.

Even thoroughly experienced owners use reasonable caution in approaching strange docks. Make a habit of observing how the flags ashore are flying, how any anchored or moored boats are lying, and how the boats at the dock are pulling at their lines, noting whether the stern and bow lines are slack or taut. These signs will tell you the direction of the wind and current.

Getting out of a slip may be troublesome. You're handicapped if the stern is out, because you can't steer or maneuver your boat nearly so effectively in reverse as in forward. If the tidal flow is the same as you enjoyed

Pass approaching craft on the right, and keep a safe distance between boats.

This cruiser has a maneuvering advantage with its twin engines.

when entering the slip, fine. Then, with the motor running in neutral, you can allow the current to carry you out. In any case, it's always a good idea to back into a slip. Leaving a slip in forward, you'll have little trouble steering and getting in the clear, even against a swift tide or current.

Often you'll have to turn your boat within practically its own length. You can manhandle the boat around, using a paddle or boat hook, but you should learn how to do this under power. With some boats, by merely spinning the wheel hard and using a short burst of forward speed, you make the stern skid around without the boat actually forging ahead. But a larger boat isn't likely to swing in such a narrow circle. If you have twin engines, putting one in forward and the other in reverse will spin the boat. Otherwise, you back and fill. A short burst of speed in forward with the wheel at full turn will start the boat swinging. If the bow comes too close to the dock or bank, you counteract by going hard astern (spinning the wheel in the opposite direction if you have outboard or stern-drive power). A short burst of speed should suffice. Then, at the right moment, spin the wheel again and shift to forward. You may have to repeat this procedure several times to get headed right.

Observe how experienced owners often use dock lines to get their big boats in and out of tight places. We'll suppose that you want to pull away from a crowded fuel dock. You're hemmed in bow and stern by other boats, and, to make matters worse, a strong wind is blowing directly against the dock. If you lead your boat's bow line to a dock cleat off the stern of your boat, then put your engine in forward with the steering wheel turned hard to push the stern sideways away from the dock, the stern will turn into the wind. The dock line will prevent the boat from moving ahead. The line must be cast off and taken in when the stern is clear. Then you can keep on backing until you have ample room to turn and be on your way. If there isn't a dock attendant to release the line, use a doubled length with both ends made fast aboard and only the loop over the dock's cleat or pile. With

In harbor areas, observe reduced speed limits. You are responsible for damage caused by your wake.

no tension on the line, you can toss the loop clear. If the line is under strain, let go of one end and haul in on the other to get the line aboard.

Often you're up against the reverse of this situation. Wind is blowing strong off the dock, or the flow of the current keeps pushing away. You can, of course, reach the dock by going forward. The difficulty is to get the boat broadside for securing with lines. Toss the eye end of a line to the dock for making fast there. Hold the other end with a turn or two around a deck cleat, one about the mid-length of the boat. Turn the steering wheel hard, making the prop force the boat's stern towards the dock. The holding line will then cause the boat to draw closer to the dock, constantly keeping parallel with it, until you can hold it there with bow and stern lines.

In ordinary or straight running, the more your boat will maintain a straight course of its own accord, without your using the steering wheel, the less tired you'll be after making long runs. Also, the less you have to fight the wheel, the more accurately you can run a compass course. Most single-engine boats, because of the torque of the spinning propeller, tend to go to one side, requiring more or less constant attention to steering. To counteract this and to make the boat ride properly, an experienced skipper will often ballast his boat by the seating arrangement of his passengers.

In rough water, your boat's behavior will largely determine how you should steer and how much power you should use. Another important factor is the wind's direction—whether you're bucking the waves, running with them, or traveling broadside to them. No set rules of handling apply. Conditions that could be classed as dangerous for small boats may be perfectly safe for a somewhat larger boat with an experienced crew. You must get to know what your boat will and won't safely do. You must learn that when waves reach the point of hindering your progress against them, you can make better time and be more comfortable by taking them on either bow rather than head-on. Also, with all boats, there can come the time when it's wise to reduce your speed.

Boating after dark is attractive for several reasons. First of all, any body of water is likely to be more or less deserted after sundown. Fishing will pick up for most species in the evening and there'll be far less activity to disturb their feeding.

In addition to almost doubling your number of fishing hours and boating activity, you can also literally double your fishing range. Any sizable body of water is likely to have its distant areas that are too time consuming to reach by day. But by making the return trip after dark you can get in enough fishing to justify the long runs.

Night fishing needn't necessarily mean merely rowing or motoring out a short distance from shore and anchoring. Night use of boats can mean running lengthy distances to and from hot fishing spots or returning from a day or weekend of exploring, and possibly camping out, with your boat. Indeed, in certain respects, the larger the body of water, the more attractive night boating may be.

The initial requirement for making night boating safe and enjoyable is to have your craft suitably equipped and to gradually gain know-how and confidence in yourself. Most boats—even the smaller ones—now come with the required basic equipment. That is, all or most of the government-required items are included. Proper lights, the right type and size for your boat, are essential. Don't overlook the importance of a proper anchor light. Night boating's greatest hazard is unlighted or inadequately lighted boats anchored or drifting in fishing areas, particularly in narrow waterways and channels. The anchor light, a white one, must be displayed when the boat is anchored and the running lights are off.

Lights other than the required ones are meant for occasional use. A powerful flashlight, or a permanently mounted small searchlight on the forward deck, is handy. If you make long runs or use your boat on wide waters at night, such a light is almost a must for spotting markers, searching out floating obstructions, or identifying stretches of shoreline, and so on. But you must not run with it on constantly. One of the worst boating practices is to turn the beam of a strong light directly on an oncoming boat, temporarily blinding its operator. The less one exposes his eyes to artificial light at night the better his natural vision will be. Even a small flashlight shouldn't be used more than necessary.

You may find that you want extra equipment. Binoculars, preferably 7 x 50's with a good nighttime rating, are even more useful at night than during the day. The same applies to some of the new electronic aids. Even a rowboat can now use a small depth finder to locate favorite fishing holes. Other aids of this nature, notably direction finders, radio telephones, and citizens-band radios, are available in small-size models, and the prices on such equipment are continually being made more attractive.

Back into a slip when possible. You then have maximum control when you pull out.

On many waters, night fishing calls for a change of tactics, different techniques, different lures, and so on. There are many little things you can do. For example, to avoid using that vision-destroying flashlight, you can use luminous tape or paint on items, such as the tackle box, handle of the landing net, even the oar handles, to make them easier to find.

The rules of daytime seamanship hold true at night, even more so. If you're a newcomer, you should learn the basic rules during the day, delaying night use until you've gained some experience. The same applies to navigational aids—buoys and other markers. Such aids will supplement your chart and compass, helping you to determine position and direction. Two important points in night boating are: 1. Always know where you are. 2. Always know what you are doing. A third requirement, which will keep even a beginner safe, is always use common sense.

As dark comes and landmarks start disappearing, note your position on the chart and determine from it any shore and buoy lights you can use to steer by.

Your eyes can play tricks at night. It's always difficult to estimate distance from shore, especially if the land is high. The same applies to entering an unlighted docking area. Rather than staring in the direction of an object or light you're trying to find, fix your eyes at a point at either side of it and it may show up. Or, rather than staring in that one direction, look around, or even close your eyes for a minute or so. Then a look in the right direction, and the object or light most likely will materialize.

COPING WITH THE WEATHER

The boat owner thinks of bad weather chiefly in terms of strong winds and the waves they create. Fog can make matters worse, of course, but is less likely to bother you. Rain can cut your visibility if it comes down hard enough; otherwise it's merely an inconvenience.

The larger the body of water, the greater sweep the wind can have and the more waves will be created. Ordinarily, the bigger the boat, the more seaworthy it will be. Its speed and dependability also help determine how well your boat will stand up to bad weather.

While you should avoid unnecessary encounters with bad weather, it's prudent to learn what to do if you're caught in it. Experience helps. As you gain boating savvy, you also acquire some weather knowledge. As you learn to handle your boat well, you get to know how far it can be trusted as well as how to steer it and what speed to use under adverse conditions. Almost any husky, well-built small boat that's reasonably well-handled will withstand far worse weather than you're likely to tackle by choice. After all, you try to avoid bad weather not only to play safe, but also to be decently comfortable.

You should consider not only what the weather is but also what it's likely to be later in the day or in the weekend. If it's blowing hard, either stay ashore or seek out water that is less affected.

What you must be on guard against are sudden weather changes for the worse. Thunderstorms, particularly those known as afternoon squalls, are

Coast Guard warning flags. Left, daytime hurricane warning, winds 72 m.p.h. and up: two flags, red background, black squares. Right, daytime small-craft warning, winds to 38 m.p.h.: red flag. Red and white lights are night signals.

your greatest hazard. Line storms—those major blows often lasting several days—do less damage to small boats. For one thing, they're quite accurately forecast, and you aren't likely to go out in the face of such warnings. Their wind speed increases gradually, giving enough time to boatmen who are out to get in before conditions get truly bad. Hurricanes, with odd exceptions, are forecast well in advance, and their sky and atmospheric indications are unmistakable to the seasoned boatman. Their chief hazard is to boats kept in the water. Owners of such craft should heed a hurricane warning by moving them to the safest, best protected spots available.

A hard summer squall can unleash many violent elements. Several inches of rain may fall in a few minutes. Even hailstones may fall. Driving rain may cut visibility to practically nil. Winds may reach 60 m.p.h. or more. Lightning may flash several times a minute.

If you think a squall's coming, you can keep running a big outboard in area that's close to shelter.

You can't expect such storms to be predicted in a weather report; generally summer squalls are local disturbances. The mere caution, "possible afternoon thunderstorms," may mean little. If you always heeded such warnings, you'd get little use from your boat. The thing to do is learn the reputation of your section and of any distant ones where you may use your boat.

Your first clue to afternoon squalls is abnormally high temperature and humidity. Watch the westerly quarter for rapidly growing cumulus clouds, with the rolling air mass darkening and growing angrier looking. Thunder is often heard half an hour to an hour before the storm strikes. If you have a radio aboard, static of the "crash" type is one of your indications. Any wind that has been blowing is likely to drop away, and usually there's a breathless calm just before the strong wind hits.

To guard against running into major weather disturbances find out what radio station or other source gives the most reliable weather forecasts for

If forced to ride out a squall, head your boat into it at reduced speed.

your section. Don't, however, trust such forecasts implicitly concerning squalls; do your own observing of sky conditions.

Try to gain boat-handling experience gradually—and as painlessly as possible. Limit any chances you take to those of your own choosing rather than getting caught unawares. During this learning stage, and even later, don't deliberately tackle bad weather with a lot of guests aboard; panic is responsible for a big percentage of boating mishaps.

It's sensible to rely somewhat on your boat's speed. If a squall seems to be making up, shift closer in, fishing where a short, fast run can put you in shelter.

In rough water, keep weight low and don't allow water to collect in bottom.

If you must ride out a hard squall or make a long run home against rising wind, prepare your boat and crew for what's coming. If your boat has a canopy or shelter, get it down and fasten it securely, even though it means the rain will get at you. Next, be concerned about getting water out of the boat. The self bailer you ordinarily depend on may not work under such conditions, particularly if you have to take waves at reduced speed. So have a hand pump stowed aboard for such an emergency. Even a hand bailer or bucket handled by a fishing buddy will allow you to concentrate more fully on your job of steering.

In a really hard blow, keep everyone low. Even a canoe will bring its crew through if two precautions are observed: 1. Sit on the bottom rather than on the seats. 2. Don't let water collect in the bottom.

Finally, think of your comfort as well as your safety. Just because the day has been hot, don't make the mistake of wearing merely shorts or a bathing suit in a squall. You'll be chilled by the combination of wind, rain, and possibly hail. Even for heavy spray, have proper wet-weather clothing stowed aboard. Buy dependable gear, and choose trousers and hooded jacket rather than a long slicker or ordinary raincoat.

19   Traffic Rules

To BE SAFE afloat today, you must know what the correct and accepted procedures are for any situation involving two or more boats operating in close quarters. That means you must have a good working knowledge of what are known as Rules of the Road at Sea. They're nothing more than traffic rules for boats, comparable in some respects with traffic rules for automobiles, and intended for the same purpose—to prevent accidents.

Though, strictly speaking, the rules apply to federal waters, including the Great Lakes and the larger navigable rivers, they're also the pattern for most state and local boating regulations.

Masters of ocean-going vessels and commercial craft have always religiously observed the rules, and so have owners of inboard pleasure craft and the larger sailboats. But outboarders, years ago, paid little heed to them. There wasn't much need to do so since outboard boats weren't numerous, were usually small and slow, and did most of their putt-putting in shallow, well-protected backwaters.

Today small-boat owners are no longer a minority group. Their craft outnumber yacht-type inboards, and many of them are big enough and fast enough to share larger bodies of open water with heavy-tonnage ships. Their owners are in the big-league now, and are expected to know the rules and to observe them.

There are only a few of them and they're simple, but everyone should know them so well that he can apply them almost instinctively in emergencies.

One of the first things to know is that boats tell each other what they are going to do by sounding their whistles or horns. Maybe your boat isn't required to have a whistle aboard, but those that are 16-feet or longer (Class 1) and are used on waterways under the jurisdiction of the Coast Guard must be equipped with a whistle or other sound-producing mechanical device. In any event, you should know what the basic signals mean should any of them be sounded by others especially for your benefit.

The most common whistle signs are illustrated in the sketch. In panel No. 1, the black boat intends to pass the white one on the right, so it sounds one short blast and eases over in that direction. The white boat then steers to its right, and all's well.

Whistle Signals: ONE short blast, "I am directing my course to starboard (right)"; TWO short blasts, "I am directing my course to port (left)"; THREE short blasts, "I am going astern (back)". You are required to answer these signals with identical signal to indicate understanding and agreement. FOUR or more short blasts, "I am in doubt, trouble, or distress"; all boats come to a stop or maneuver with caution.

In the panel No. 2, the big white inboard is about to enter the side channel on its left, and notifies the black outboard of its intentions by sounding two blasts. Because of its size, the inboard needs room to make the turn and then to straighten out. That's why its captain is well over on the far side of the channel marked by the buoys. Knowing what the inboard is about to do, the outboard moves to the left side of the channel, slows down, and stops if necessary until the white boat completes its maneuver. The three little black bars indicate about where the outboard would stop if it had to.

In panel No. 3, the large white inboard sounding three blasts is telling the other two boats coming down the channel that it is backing up—going astern. Most likely it's pulling off a shoal. So the two boats slow down or stop, giving the larger boat plenty of room in which to maneuver.

In panel No. 4, a tug with a barge in tow is getting its towline straightened out before attempting to pass under the opened bridge. That takes some doing and requires plenty of room. The tug captain sounds four blasts to warn craft on the other side of the bridge. He may sound more than four if he deems it necessary. What he's saying, in effect, is: "I may have a bit of trouble here, so watch out. Give me room. Stand by until I'm through."

Responding to the signal, the white outboard has moved well over to the left and stopped, and the black outboard is about to go astern of it and stop. Both will be well clear of the deep-water channel by the time the tug and its tow pass under the bridge and make the turn.

In addition to the signals illustrated, you should know that one prolonged blast means that a ship is leaving its dock or slip. It is warning you to keep out of its way.

In foggy weather, boats signal their presence by sounding one prolonged blast every minute. By keeping track of the blasts—their intensity and changing direction—you usually can figure where the boat is and judge how best to steer clear of it. If the prolonged blast is followed by a couple of shorter ones, it means that the vessel has something in tow—most likely a barge. Then you must watch out not only for the vessel but for its tow and also for the long cable or hawser connecting the two.

Boats also use whistles or horns to request drawing or lifting of bridges and canal locks. Small boats rarely need to sound these signals, but it's well to know that, where warranted, three blasts are blown for a bridge to open, generally four when approaching a lock.

As you can see, horn blowing on the water isn't like horn blowing on the highways. The number and nature of the blasts have a definite meaning. That's why no responsible boat owner ever honks just because he's impatient, angry, or wants to make a noise. All signals should be given with a definite purpose and answered with a like signal or with a distress signal.

Often you can be on the water day after day and sound your horn only once or twice—sometimes not at all. A knowledge of the other basic traffic rules makes this possible.

When you're approaching another boat head-on or nearly so, the customary thing for both boats to do is swing to the right, pass, then straighten out on their original courses. In open water this may not be necessary.

Large vessels approaching head-on would signal their intentions of keeping to the right by blowing a signal blast, one replying to the other, but small craft seldom find that necessary. It's a good idea, though, to start turning off course well in advance of passing so that the other fellow will know what you're going to do.

When you wish to overtake another boat, it is permissible to do so either on the left or right. Always bear in mind, however, that the boat you are overtaking is what is known as the "privileged" boat and has the right of way. Its captain may indicate which side he wants you to pass on, and you must respect his wishes.

When you're overtaking, give the other fellow plenty of room, be conscious of your wake, and don't dawdle. Don't zoom by at top speed, either, especially if the boat you're passing is a small one. Your wake may toss it violently, perhaps dangerously. It's never wise to run parallel to a heavy wake for any length of time, for it will tend to throw your boat heavily and may possibly pitch it out of control.

For a while, novices sometimes have a little trouble remembering who

THE BOATMAN'S RULES OF THE ROAD

1. When boats approach head-on, each alters course to right to pass. Proper signal is one toot from either boat, answered by one toot from the other.

2. Boat traveling with current or tide has right of way through span, but this small boat wisely gives big commercial craft wide berth, letting it pass first.

3. When overtaking, the passing boat sig-

nals one blast to pass on the right, two blasts for left. If boat does not answer with same signals, do not pass.

4. This boat is violating two rules: it's tied to a navigational buoy and obstructing traffic in channel.

5. If you're new at boating, do your learning in the quiet stretches. Expose yourself to traffic gradually.

142

6. Outboard slows when passing canoe. Same applies for any small boat that could be endangered by wake.

7. Sailboat traveling entirely under sail has the right of way. The outboard changes its course to go behind it.

8. Legally, ferry should wait for boat to pass slip. This outboarder, however, is wisely waiting for the big difficult-to-maneuver craft to clear the dock.

9. Outboard cuts speed to reduce wake as it passes boats at dock. The same courtesy applies when power craft pass any anchored, moored, or drifting boat.

10. Whenever two boats are about to cross each other, the one having the other on her own right side (A) keeps out of the way, lets the other one (B) go ahead.

should do what when they want to cross the path of another boat that's approaching them either at right angles or on a slant. It's simple. The boat that has the other one on its right must slow down, stop, reverse, or alter its course, whichever seems called for under the circumstances. The other boat, which has the right of way, goes ahead.

The reason for this is that the privileged boat is in what's known as the burdened boat's "danger zone." Technically this is defined as "from dead ahead to two points abaft the starboard beam." For all practical purposes, the zone may be considered as taking in the forward two-thirds of your right direction.

Those are the basic rules. Knowing when to apply them is important; so is knowing when not to apply them. It would be foolish, for example, for a small boat to assert its right of way and insist that an ocean liner change its course. The same goes for all large vessels, commercial fishing craft, and tugs with tows. It's good sense to stay clear of them since their high bows and special deck equipment often makes it difficult for their officers and men to see near-by small boats.

Sailboats almost always have the right of way over powered vessels. They should be given a wide berth, especially when they're participating in races.

Remember that you are responsible for any damage your wake may cause, so throttle down when you're passing rowboats and canoes and when running close to anchored craft, little or big. Don't anchor in or hog the middle of narrow, busy waterways. Never tie up at a channel marker or other aid to navigation, and be on the lookout for skiers, skindivers and for swimmers when you're close to beaches.

These last few do's and don'ts aren't included in the Rules of the Road but most have long been respected by boat owners just because they make sense and are the courteous things to do. They all add up to greater safety and more pleasure for everyone afloat.

20 Getting There and Back

IF YOU are going to use your boat only on a pond or a stream, always within a shout of shore, you will have no real need to learn anything about piloting or navigating. If, however, you find it a challenge, or if you get caught up in the trend to bigger and faster boats, with larger bodies of water beckoning, then you owe it to yourself and to your trusting companions to learn something of basic piloting—or how to get to a distant point on the water and get back to your point of departure safely despite weather conditions.

One way to learn piloting is to take a course in boat handling conducted by organizations such as the U. S. Power Squadrons or the Coast Guard Auxiliary. But if you must learn piloting on your own, there are several good books you can study, and sometimes you can get an experienced friend to help you.

If you use your boat on fairly large, open bodies of water, you'll find that government charts of the area, or their equivalents, are probably available locally. These charts are much more accurate than road maps. Nothing on them is distorted, and the locations of buoys, shorelines, shoals, wrecks, and other features are accurately marked. Prominent objects on shore, such as water tanks and towers, are clearly shown. Depths of the water are given, and the nature of the bottom is indicated—M. for mud, Oz. for ooze, Sh. for shells, S. for sand, and so on. You'll soon acquire a good, general knowledge of the nature of any body of water by studying a chart of it.

Printed on every government chart is the compass rose. It is important, for it is the means by which you determine what direction to steer your boat to get from one point to another shown on the chart. In the rough sketch of the chart shown, the compass rose is the object, at top, consisting of two graduated circles. Compass directions are given on the circles by numbers which indicate degrees. On the outer circle, North is 0°, and, going clockwise, East is 90°, South 180°, and West 270°. The full circle is 360°. The inner circle is similarly marked. The difference between the circles is that the outer one represents what are known as true or geographical directions, while the inner circle represents what are known as magnetic directions. When you're piloting, the inner or magnetic circle is the one you'll be interested in since you will be using a compass that points toward the magnetic North and not to the true or geographical North. There is what is known as "variation" be-

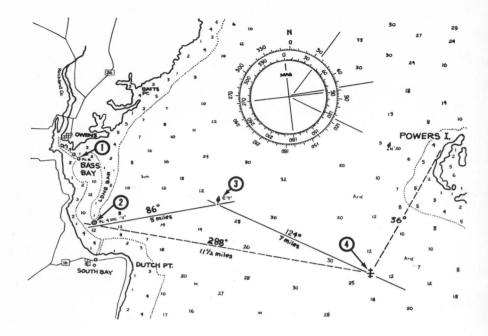

Simple chart shows piloting problem—locating submerged wreck (4). Buoy (3) provides an intermediate fixed point from which boatman takes compass bearings.

tween the two, but that need not concern us right now. It is something you will learn more about later if you decide to become a competent pilot.

The compass you will be using on your boat in conjunction with the chart and its compass rose should be properly mounted in gimbals so that the compass card indicating directions in degrees from 0 to 360 remains level and free to turn despite the boat's motion. Don't mount the compass too close to the motor or the place where you stow your anchor or other metal objects. The metal will throw the compass off and make its readings unreliable. A compass should be mounted at least 4 feet away from any large piece of metal.

Let's say that you want to fish the wreck located at point 4 on the sketch of the chart. You'll plot your course before you start out from the boat-launching site at 1, inside Bass Bay. You'll have to keep clear of that long, shallow bar sheltering the bay, but that's just a matter of keeping an eye out for shoal water and running along the shore until you arrive at the fixed marker at the southern end of the bar, marked 2.

Since the wreck at 4 is a considerable distance away, you better your chances of locating it by steering for a dependable marker at some intermediate spot. Fortunately, the chart shows that there's a buoy about midway to the wreck's location but somewhat to the north of the direct course. To determine your compass course to reach the buoy, first draw a line on the chart from 2 to the buoy at 3. The next step is to find how many degrees you'll have to steer to reach the buoy.

Here's where the compass rose comes in. It will tell you how many degrees to steer, and to get it to do so you use a pair of parallel rulers like the ones shown in the small drawing.

Parallel rules consist of two rulers held together with hinged bars so that the edges of the rulers are always parallel, though the rulers may be closed or opened. Place the outside edge of the lower ruler on the course line from 2 to 3 and move, or "walk" the outside edge of the other ruler across the chart until that ruler cuts across the center dot in the compass rose. Now draw a line from the center dot through the rim of the compass rose. This line crosses the *inner* circle of numbers at 86°, as shown in the illustration. That is your compass course to the buoy. Steer the bow of your boat around until your compass indicates 86° and you'll be on course. There are devices other than parallel rules that may be used in plotting a course, for example course protractors and finders.

After reaching the buoy at 3, you'll need a new course bearing to get to the submerged wreck. Draw a line from the buoy to the symbol representing the wreck, at 4, and use your parallel rules to determine the new course. As shown on the sketch of the chart, the second bearing is 124°, but since the wreck is entirely underwater and the chart does not show a marker buoy over it, you won't know when you've arrived at it unless you use other piloting techniques.

Before attempting to run a course, be sure you know your boat's normal cruising speed in land miles per hour and nautical miles since either measure may be used on a chart. A nautical mile is slightly longer than a land mile (6076 feet, nautical; 5280 feet, statute). In our example, let's say that your normal cruising speed is 12 nautical miles an hour or 1 mile every five minutes. The scale of miles on the chart shows that it's 7 miles from the buoy to the wreck. Since you cover a mile every five minutes, you should reach the wreck in about thirty five minutes.

Unless you can see the wreck in the water, you will have to start taking soundings to locate it. Traditionally, this is done by lowering a length of line weighted with a hunk of lead, possibly a sinker, on the end of it. Some-

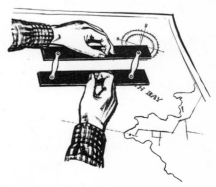

Parallel rules used in laying a course.

times the difference in the water's color over a large submerged object such as a wreck or a reef will clue you in. If you can't locate your objective right away, the current or the wind may have thrown you somewhat off course. If your piloting has been fairly accurate, you can be sure that you're close.

There are several ways to check your position in relation to a submerged object. Knowing the depth of the water helps. Our sample chart shows that the water to the north and east of the wreck is much shallower than the area west and south of it. By checking the depth of the water with a weighted line, you'll get a good idea of your position. If your lead line shows that the water is 30 feet deep, you can be pretty sure that you're west of the wreck. If the water is only 7 feet deep, you can bet you're east of it. By jockeying your boat around and checking the depth frequently, you should be able to zero in reasonably quickly.

Taking a bearing on some fixed point that you can see on land may help. The chart shows that there's a group of island to the northward that should be visible as you approach the wreck. Your chart, parallel rules, and compass rose will tell you that the western edge of the largest island should bear 36° away when you arrive over the wreck, as shown by the dotted line on the chart. By watching the degree markings on your compass as you approach while steering 124°, you have another good indication of the spot where you should stop.

To get back from the wreck to your launching site, you can steer the reverse of your outbound courses. To determine the reverse of any compass course, simply add to or subtract from it 180° as required. Hence, to get back from the wreck at 4 to buoy at 3, steer a course of 124° plus 180°, that is 304°. To get from the buoy at 3 to the marker at 2, steer a course of 86° plus 180°, that is 266°. Then you make your way back up the shoreline to your launching site at 1.

Instead of running these two courses, you may decide you'd like to run directly from the wreck at 4 to the marker at 2. If so, draw a line between those points, get out your parallel rulers, and walk them up to the compass rose. You'll find that the course is 288°.

If when you approach the shore you find that visibility is bad and you can't recognize any landmarks, stop and take some soundings with your lead line. By comparing these soundings with the depths indicated on the chart, you may be able to get a good idea of how far you are from the beach.

In this example of simple piloting, you used a known running speed to determine your location. In fog or darkness, you will be operating your boat at slower speeds than you do in clear weather or daylight. Because of this, it's a good idea to know how fast your boat moves at, say, half its normal cruising speed. In this case, cruising speed was a mile every five minutes. At half that, it will take ten minutes to cover a mile. In returning directly from the wreck, the running time at this low speed would be a little less than two hours since the distance is 11½ miles. You'd note the exact time when leaving the wreck and then keep the boat running at the half-speed throttle. Well before running your time out, you'd expect to pick up the shore and identify landmarks. Then you'd pick up the marker at the end of the long bar and steer for it. A notation on the chart tells you that the marker has a flashing light, so you should be able to locate it after dark or even if the visibility is poor. If visibility is bad when you approach the shore, be cautious.

Make certain that your compass is correct, and then trust it. By checking your compass at least twice during the season, you can accomplish two important missions—be sure that it hasn't been adversely affected by metal brought aboard or moved about and, just as important, you will gain confidence in it.

To check your compass, line up your boat, along the centerline, with a series of landmarks noted on your chart. Compare the compass reading with the magnetic bearing on the chart. Any difference is known as deviation. If you will note the amount of deviation on a permanent record, you can apply it to correct the heading every time you run your boat in that direction. By lining up your boat on a series of headings around the compass and noting the deviation, you can make a list of the variables for plotting an accurate course for your boat every time you use a chart in that general area.

Get in the habit of operating your boat in a seamanlike manner. If it is equipped with basic instruments, use them. Even in bright sunlight, plot your courses and steer by the compass as though visibility were zero. Train yourself to be observant.

You should become familiar with the speed of your boat at various r.p.m.; and you should note the affect of wind and current in pushing you off your course. Check your time in covering known distances.

There are Tide and Current Tables issued by the government. As you get more involved in the art of piloting, you will want to learn to apply the information those tables impart. However, even without them, you can observe the direction and force of water around buoys.

When planning a course on larger waters, take advantage of noisemaking navigation aids like bell buoys, and whistling buoys that are well clear of hazards. Then if you should find yourself suddenly fogbound, you'll have an additional means of establishing your location and a course to safety.

Equip your boat with a sounding line. Length should depend upon depth of waters you use. Soundings can be extremely helpful—in locating a good fishing hole; and possibly in finding your way home when lost.

You'll gradually acquire local knowledge to complement your piloting skill. In fair weather, try to observe the many seemingly unrelated details that are very useful when visibility is limited. Commercial fishermen rely largely on local knowledge, and you can use that same knowledge to improve your own fishing and to avoid danger. For instance, lobster-pot buoys are often located along rocky bottoms. When other marks are hard to see, you can often avoid trouble by staying in deep water outside a known line of buoys. Sometimes lobster pots are anchored around the edges of a ledge or rocky shoal and the buoys form a circle on the surface. Knowing the pattern helps you to avoid shoal water. On the other hand, you may be looking for one of these shoals because it offers good fishing. Oysters stakes are generally located in 10 feet or so of water on a clear-sand bottom. Crab-trap buoys or stakes often line the edges of a deep channel.

The water may be clear enough so that its color will indicate its depth and the nature of its bottom. The water over a sand bottom is usually light in color while that over mud is of a darker cast. Streamers of kelp or weed beneath the surface usually mean a rocky bottom. Eel grass indicates shallowing water. You can use these facts to locate different kinds of fish. For example, flounder like level mud in shallow water, while mackerel are usually in deeper water.

Keep the wind direction in mind and observe the wind's effects. On the Atlantic coast, fog usually comes on an easterly wind. Warm-weather haze usually lies in the southwest. Waves do not always run with the wind, but a sharp difference in the angle between wave and wind directions often indicates a current in a channel or inlet. Tide rips, races, or small wavelets imposed on the general wave pattern usually mean shallowing water. Abrupt heaving or swells in an average sea also indicate shallowing water, probably a bar or ledge. You may be trying to avoid shallow areas or you may be trying to locate a certain shallow spot so you can fish over it. Locating a shallow spot or rock also helps you in determining your position. By pinpointing the shallow area on the chart, you can plot your course from it to other points.

The actions of birds are often helpful signs. Wheeling gulls are usually feeding on small fish probably driven to the surface by larger fish. Flocks of gulls make for land in the evening and head seaward in the morning. In fog, land birds are generally flying toward the shore. At dusk, ducks head for land, often toward a cove or inlet.

21 Anchoring and Mooring

WHETHER AN anchor is just something handy to have aboard or is an important piece of equipment depends on how you use it. A chunk of iron may hold your small boat, but a modern small anchor is more convenient to use and will do a better job. Logically, the need for proper anchoring equipment and knowledge of how to use it increase in proportion to boat size. For example, a craft used for overnight trips or on open water is highly dependent on its anchoring equipment. There are bound to be times when the boat's safety and perhaps that of its owner and passengers will rest on what's used —and how.

STANDARD ANCHOR TYPES

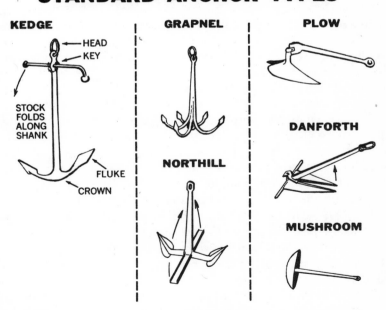

In addition to these standard types, which are available in small boat sizes, there is also a great variety of small fishing anchors.

Great progress has been made in providing miniature or lightweight versions of anchor types which are proving so satisfactory for larger craft. Outstanding examples are the Danforth, Northill, and plow anchors. In addition, a number of small-boat anchor styles have been developed, generally with some special convenience feature. For example, a few anchors for small boats are plastic-coated or encased in rubber to protect the metal against rusting and to have an anchor that is quieter to use and easier on the boat's finish. Some fishermen's anchors are also copied after some old style, frequently the mushroom type.

You can generally tell just by looking at an anchor whether it is designed to hold mainly by weight or by digging into the bottom. Small-size anchors designed to dig in, weighing about 5 pounds, can hold an average open outboard, and a 10-pounder of this type can anchor a good-size cruiser. Anchors depending on sheer weight for holding power come in heavier sizes in proportion to boat size. For example, a 15-pounder of such design is recommended for the average open outboard. For larger boats, however, it would have to be excessively heavy and the modern digging-in type of anchor by far excels these heavy designs.

What must be kept in mind when selecting an anchor is the nature of the bottom where you do your boating. Generally, an anchor's holding power depends on its ability to dig in. This is particularly true if you are over a very soft bottom. A properly designed anchor on such a bottom will be buried deeper and deeper by the pull of the boat on the anchor line until it eventual reaches bottom solid enough to give its flukes a firm grip. On the other hand, an anchor which holds largely because of its weight tends to keep dragging through the soft surface of the bottom. Even on a firm bottom, however, and in extreme cases where the bottom is hard gravel or fairly smooth rock, a well-designed lightweight anchor will—after dragging a bit—find a place where its sharp points can get a hold. What will help, with any anchor, is a 10-foot length of light chain, shackled between the anchor and line. It's also wise to use the chain rig when you're over coral or rocks sharp enough to chafe an ordinary line. Even on soft bottom, a chain will make a light anchor dig in more quickly.

Another bottom condition that may be encountered, particularly about a man-made body of water, is underwater obstructions which can snag your anchor and often make retrieving impossible. One trick is to use a trip line, a length of 1/4-inch rope a few feet longer than the depth of water. Tie one end to a small buoy or float. Then, if hauling on the regular line doesn't release the snagged anchor, pick up the buoy and pull on its line. The anchor can generally be freed and hauled up crown first.

Ordinarily, a straight-up pull on any well-designed anchor will free it. Beyond that, though, the shape of the anchor should be such that mud won't adhere to it. A few swishes through the water before lifting the anchor aboard should serve to wash it clean. You should be able to stow it where it will be out of the way, but quickly available. For salt water, an anchor should

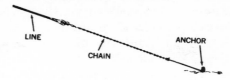

Shackling 10-foot chain between line and anchor increases hold, prevents chafing.

be hot galvanized, not just plated, against rusting. Modern anchors rate well in all these respects and are also designed to resist fouling with the anchor line, a common fault of the older types.

If any anchor is so designed that the line can wind about some part of it on a change of tide or wind, its holding power is largely destroyed. But one old style, the five-pronged grapnel, is handy to have about any dock or boathouse. It makes a fairly good fishing-boat anchor, though its main usefulness is in locating and retrieving a motor or other bulky equipment lost overboard.

Logically, an anchor is no better than the line tied to it. Age, chafe, and rot are enemies. The size of the line, within reason, isn't as important as its condition. Manila and nylon have their advantages and disadvantages, and which line is used is largely a matter of personal preference. Remember that lighter line is harder on the hands in hauling. Chafe can be guarded against by splicing the line around a metal thimble or using a shackle to attach it to an anchor chain. Make it a practice to coil your line and to stow it neatly, always in a place where the air can get to it. Also, turn the line end for end seasonally to equalize the wear and exposure.

There are now a number of reels and winches adapted to small or open boats and designed to simplify anchoring. In addition, there are lightweight versions of big-boat windlasses to take the strain out of handling the anchor on a husky outboard or inboard cruiser. The open-boat windlasses are particularly well designed and especially useful for fishing boats. Invariably, some means of taking care of the anchor line is provided, and often the operation is such that the fitting can be permanently mounted on the bow and controlled from the stern. There may be a cradle or holder to take the anchor and some means of checking the rope in paying it out.

But there is more to anchoring than just having a suitable anchor and some way of handling it. You must know how to use it for best results. The

Scope of anchor line is an important holding factor. A. Sufficient for ordinary fishing. B. Increase line if wind builds up. C. For strong winds or overnight anchoring, length is up to seven times depth of water.

first thing to realize is that an anchor's holding power depends on the scope or length of line that's let out. If only enough is released so that the line runs nearly straight down to the anchor, the holding power will be poor. Letting out a length of line from five to seven times the depth of water is the rule for giving an anchor sufficient scope. That means if you're anchoring in 5 feet of water, at least 25 to 35 feet of line should extend between the boat and the anchor to have it hold effectively. Increasing this length will give better holding under extreme conditions and often cause the boat to ride easier in rough water.

What counts, of course, is not only the direction of the wind but where a change in the wind will place your craft. For overnight anchoring, try to pick a spot offering the shelter of some point of land or even a patch of marsh from your most open quarter, where a wind could get its greatest sweep at you over open water. A lee shore, where a wind could blow over an open expanse to put you aground, is particularly bad because of the waves that could build up. Also bad is an anchorage from which dragging could put you down on rocks or pilings.

The wrong way to do the job is to merely toss the anchor overboard with most of its line. That's sure to result in the line getting fouled around the anchor and destroying its holding power. Instead, make it a practice to lower the anchor at the bow while the motor is running in neutral. Keep the line under control until the anchor hits the bottom making sure the line comes off the top of the coil so it doesn't foul. Then, as the wind or current starts to carry the boat away from the anchor, let out line gradually to give the anchor a chance to dig in. In calm weather, you can back away with the motor in reverse to dig in the anchor.

A well-designed anchor should come out easily when the line is pulled straight up. If an anchor is firmly set, however, as might happen in a hard blow, the lift of the waves can be utilized. Move directly over the anchor, get in as much line as possible, and snub it taut about the bitt or cleat on the deck. The buoyancy of the bow as it is lifted by the waves should exert enough pull to gradually work the anchor loose. Or you can use the motor to exert a strain on the line and worry the anchor loose. However, this can be done safely only with a heavy, stable boat. With a light craft, there is always the chance that the snubbed bow will list the boat badly or even capsize it.

It is important to always have the bitter or inboard end of your anchor line permanently secured to a ring on the bow, a ringbolt inside the stem, or spliced about the base of the cleat on the forward deck. Otherwise you may one day suffer the helpless feeling of finding that the end has been pulled through your hands just when you want your anchoring to be most effective.

Another use for your anchor comes after you've beached your boat. Make it a habit to carry the anchor ashore to hook or bury it so that the wind or current can't wash the boat free. This is usually more practical than tying a bowline to a tree or snag. In tidal waters, remember to take the fluctuation of the water level into consideration. If the tide is falling, heave the anchor well out to allow for the receding water. On a rising tide, carry it well up on the beach so that the boat can float in to it to avoid your having to wade out.

Also, when drift fishing with the current, you may want to use your anchor to regulate your speed over the bottom. A type that holds largely because of its weight may be best to use in this situation, since any other design is apt to catch on some bottom obstruction.

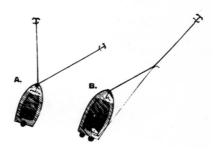

Two methods of steadying a roaming boat: A. Add second anchor. B. Tie light line to anchor line, then to a stern cleat. Adjust lines until boat rides properly in the water.

If all you have is an anchor that is made to dig into the bottom, you can still use it for drift fishing if it is altered slightly. Simply double your line back on the shank of the anchor and lash it to the crown. The ordinary holding power of your anchor will be destroyed, and you will be dependent on the length of line payed out. That is, shortening the line will allow the boat to drift with the current, paying out a little more line will slow up its drift, and giving it plenty of scope will stop the boat when you find a place where you want to make several casts.

Similarly, in lake or pond fishing when you're anchored but want to change position, it's just a matter of picking your spot first with the direction of the wind in mind. Then, by adjusting the scope of the anchor line, you can drift, as slowly as you wish, across the likeliest patch of bottom.

HOW TO PUT DOWN A MOORING

Putting down a heavy anchor with a buoy as a permanent mooring or driving a stake on which to moor your boat has several advantages over keeping it alongside a dock. It's usually simpler and much cheaper than building a dock, and rental fees for space are either nonexistent or small when compared with the amounts charged for dockside footage. In some places, zoning regulations make it difficult or impossible to build a dock, but that is rarely the case with moorings. If you like to spend time aboard on weekends without moving your boat, a mooring gives you privacy. Of course, if your mooring's some distance away from shore, you'll have to make provision for a tender to put you aboard and take you off. Many boatmen with larger rigs carry small tenders primarily for this purpose, and marinas, clubs, and boat liveries often maintain tender service.

If you don't own waterfront property, you'll have to find a suitable location. For a small fee, farmers with fields bordering on the water often will allow you to put down a mooring and drive to and from the shore. There is one small fishing club which put a farmer in the marina business. The club first got permission to put in half a dozen moorings, and then a small dock was built as a landing. The farmer's son keeps an eye on the boats, and the members often pay a bit extra to have them cleaned or painted.

There are two main types of permanent moorings—stakes and anchors. Stakes are usually used for small boats up to about 20 feet, and heavy anchors are used for larger craft. The bottom must be soft enough to permit driving a stake, but it must be firm enough to give the stake a proper hold. Over very hard bottom and rock, or very soft, soupy bottom, it's best to use an anchor.

TO DRIVE A PILE

If you decide on a stake, a green, hardwood sapling or small tree is far superior to most lumberyard stock. Oak and hickory saplings are excellent. For extra holding power, drive a tight cluster of stakes and lash their heads together, as shown in the drawing.

Ordinarily, the bark is left on mooring stakes. A skinned stake can be very slippery to handle, and in salt water the bark slows down marine borers. Above water, the stake can be peeled after it's driven or this can be done as the bark starts to flake off naturally.

PILING CLUSTER

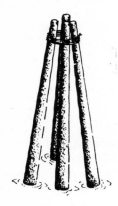

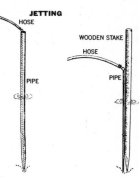

Several stakes with tops lashed together make a solid, secure mooring rig.

Water from hose flushes mud away to sink stake. Left, hose inside pipe used as stake. Right, pipe is temporarily secured to wooden stake with bent nails or cord.

The stake or pile should be driven big end down. Usually the bottom end is pointed, but if small rocks will be encountered, a wedge shape makes for straighter driving. The length of the stake must allow for the depth of the water, the soft mud or sand, and several feet of penetration into the harder material underneath, plus four feet or more above water. The top end should be thick enough to withstand the hammering.

You can drive stakes with a sledge hammer or homemade maul. Work from a boat that puts you high enough above the water so that you can really swing your hammer. If necessary, steady the boat by putting out a couple of anchors, and stand on a stout packing case steadied by a helper. Better still, connect two skiffs, as shown in the drawing. The boats should be secured just far enough apart to hold the pile or stake between them.

Shove the stake through the soft mud and start hammering when it hits harder material. Don't stop until the stake is as far in as it will go. The bottom tends to grip the stake if you stop hammering, and this makes further penetration difficult or impossible.

Hiring a commercial pile-driving rig is usually expensive, but such rigs sink heavy, creosoted piles that last a long time. Sometimes you can get the work done cheaply, however, if the pile driver is operating nearby and your work can be fitted between other jobs.

Jetting is another practical way to put in a stake if water under pressure is available. If not, you can sometimes borrow a hand force pump and use water from overside. Connect the discharge end of the hose to a long length of $\frac{3}{8}$-inch or $\frac{1}{2}$-inch pipe. The pipe and the stake are fastened together in a way permitting removal of the pipe after the stake is driven. Drive a few long nails into the stake and bend them over the pipe, but leave the pipe free enough so that it can be pulled out vertically. Or you can lash the pipe to the stake with twine light enough to break when you wrench the pipe free. Ordinary hose pressure should suffice to wash away the bottom ahead of the stake. As shown in the drawing, you can also use a fairly heavy pipe as the stake. Hammer the end of the pipe into a rough point, but leave a small opening through which the jet of water passes. Run your hose inside the pipe. With pipes or wooden stakes, hammering the top end helps even when you're using a water jet. It takes several weeks for the disturbed bottom to settle back and grip the stake firmly.

STAKE-DRIVING PLATFORM

Anchored skiffs lashed together make
driving simple.

However you drive a stake, don't be worried if at first the head can be moved back and forth. Because of the grip of the bottom, and the suction, a well-driven stake will eventually root itself firmly enough to withstand considerable strain.

Commercial fishermen often sink heavy stakes for pound nets by jiggling them. A sharpened stake is upended and forcefully dropped into position.

SIMPLE STAKE MOORING

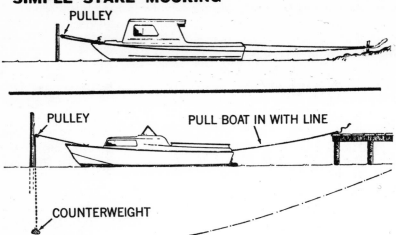

Rope and pulley allow boat to be pulled to the shore (top). As tide rises and falls, counterweight keeps rope taut (bottom).

Using a heavy chain, the fishermen then attach a slimmer pole as a crosspiece, and two men jump up and down on it to drive the stake in. A helper in a boat meanwhile moves one end of the crosspiece back and forth to grind away at the bottom.

If you find it possible to drive your stake fairly close to shore, you can use a line-and-pulley arrangement to haul the boat to you so that you can step aboard from the beach. The drawings show two methods of rigging the mooring. If the water's deep and there's considerable tidal rise and fall, use a weight below the pulley on the stake to take up and release line as the water level changes.

If the stake must be located fairly far from shore, simply tie your boat to it, provided there's no tide. If the water level does change, use a floating ring or square wooden frame. As the sketches show, the stake runs through the ring or frame. The mooring line is fastened to the float which is free to move up and down with the tide.

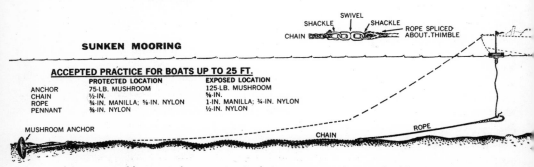

Lower part of heavy sunken mooring is chain, upper part is rope. In this case, rope pennant is used to haul in mooring line.

TO SINK A PERMANENT ANCHOR

You can use a block of concrete or a junked automobile engine as the anchor in rigging a permanent, submerged mooring. You can also use a mushroom anchor rigged in the traditional way shown in the drawing. With a concrete block or an engine, you're largely dependent on sheer weight for holding power, and of course any object weighs less when submerged. As the weight sinks deeper into the mud or sand, however, it will hold better.

Rope deteriorates quickly when permanently submerged, and you should be very careful about using it in all submerged moorings. Fitting a large ring securely to the concrete block or engine helps. Run the mooring rope through the ring and use it doubled. When the rope begins to wear out, tie on a new length and pull it through the ring with the old rope. With a doubled rope running through the ring, you can replace the line without raising the anchor.

STAKE FLOATS

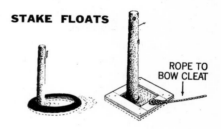

ROPE TO
BOW CLEAT

A wooden frame or old tire casing full of flotation material rises and falls with change in tides.

A mushroom anchor's shape rather than weight provides most of its holding power, but any anchor used for a permanent mooring should be considerably heavier than the one ordinarily used with the boat for temporary anchoring.

The best underwater moorings are rigged with a combination of chain and rope arranged as shown in the drawing. Using chain for the entire length would make the mooring too heavy and difficult to handle, and chain is difficult to secure to the boat without damaging paint and woodwork. A long, sunken mooring rigged entirely with rope would require replacement of the entire length too frequently. Chain retains its strength indefinitely, and its weight increases holding power. The greater the pull on the mooring, the more chain straightens out and lifts off the bottom. The length of rope attached to the chain is easy to replace when it wears out since you don't have to lift the anchor. Simply haul in the rope until you reach the swivel and shackle on new rope. During the winter, if your boat is laid up ashore, remove the pickup buoy and the rope, and replace them with old line and a block of wood. All that's needed is a means of locating and picking up the chain come spring.

The pickup buoy is important. If the buoy is meant to be hauled aboard your boat, it should be light in weight and small enough so that in an emergency your wife or child can handle it while you're maneuvering the boat.

HOMEMADE BUOY

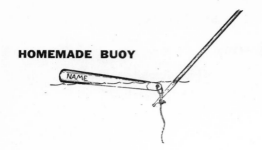

PATENT BOATHOOK HEAD

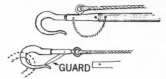

Simple wooden buoy is taken aboard the boat with ordinary boathook.

Shaft pulls out of "automatic" boathook once hook is through eye or ring. Guard snaps shut.

The homemade buoy in the drawing is one of the simplest. Buoys that are left in the water are usually heavier and larger. With this type of buoy, the line leading to the anchor is usually attached to one end and the rope pennant leading to the boat is attached to the other. The pennant's free end is spliced into an eye, and this is picked up and dropped over the bow cleat when you're mooring your boat.

The drawing of the submerged mooring shows another way of buoying a heavy mooring. The buoy is lightweight and has a staff that projects a few feet above the water. When you approach the buoy, someone pulls the buoy aboard by the staff. A light line, also called a pennant, runs from the bottom of the buoy to the eye spliced in the heavy mooring rope. The eye is hauled in and dropped over a cleat.

Sometimes it's difficult to pick up the mooring pennant or buoy. This is particularly true when you're alone and must also handle the wheel. The patented boathook head shown in the drawing makes this task easier. It works like the flying gaff used by fishermen. The shaft of the boathook pulls out of the head once the hook is through the eye splice of the mooring pennant or the ring on the buoy. To use this type of boathook, one end of a light line is secured to the bow cleat and the other end is secured to the ring on the boathook's head. Once the pennant or buoy ring is hooked, the wooden shaft is pulled free and a guard or bail snaps across the hook opening so that it will not come free. This leaves the boat temporarily secured until the heavy mooring line or the pennant can be conveniently hauled aboard.

A secure mooring gives a boat owner considerable peace of mind, and that's return enough on the investment. However, your anchor or your mooring is only as strong as the line you are using.

KNOW YOUR ROPES

We now have a wider choice of ropes than ever before, and, equally important, it has become easier to get good rope at reasonable prices. For one thing, there are more marine dealers stocking the proper ropes for boating. Moreover, their prices are being held down by companies selling direct to the individual by mail. Mail-order buying is often preferable in isolated sections where dealers' stocks may be incomplete or prices badly out of line.

Before we go on, let's take a minute to consider proper terminology. First of all, a rope is called a rope or cordage when it's in a coil in the dealer's stockroom. Once aboard a boat, a length of rope becomes a line. That is, you refer to anchor lines, dock lines, bow line, stern line, and so on.

When buying rope, there are two factors to consider: 1. Where and how you plan to use it, which determines the length and type of rope to buy. 2. The size of your boat, which sets the diameter necessary for the job.

Various types of rope are best compared if first divided into two broad groups: 1. Ropes of natural fiber, mainly Manila hemp, sisal, and cotton. 2. Synthetic ropes, such as nylon, Dacron, polyethylene, and polypropylene. There are other combination types, usually carrying a brand name, which are also classified as synthetics.

In the first group, sisal and cotton are no longer worth consideration. Sisal, which looks enough like Manila to be sometimes passed off for it, is the cheapest rope for boating. But it should not be used where strength and durability are important. Sisal rope is weaker than Manila, more brittle, tends to be pricklier, and is more readily affected by cold temperatures and moisture. It deteriorates even more rapidly than Manila from the effects of dampness and poor ventilation in storage.

Cotton rope, which in the better grades can be confused with nylon, is soft, easy to handle, and lacks those irritating whiskers. Its breaking strain, however, is much lower than Manila. Cotton rope must be stored dry to last, and even then it has a comparatively short life.

Manila, by far the best of this the natural-fiber group, comes in a range of grades, from commercial to yacht quality. The difference, which is set by the length and quality of the individual fibers, will be apparent in fingering the new rope and will become more and more apparent in actual service. A satisfactory grade will cost about 3¢ to 5¢ per foot for 1/4-inch diameter, 5 1/2¢ to 8¢ for 3/8 inch, 9¢ to 12¢ for 1/2 inch. The breaking strain for 1/4 inch is rated 600 pounds, and the average weight per 100 feet is 1.96 pounds. The good or better grades should be supple and smooth to handle as compared with the stiffer, poorer grades. Since the fibers are softer and longer, whisker shed shouldn't be as irritating. Splicing Manila is simple once you've gotten onto it, and knots and hitches hold well. It tends to kink while new, particularly when wet. One remedy is to wet the line and stretch it tightly between two trees or posts to dry. Manila is subject to rot and mildew, and, even though it is often treated with a preservative, should be thoroughly dry before storing in a dry, ventilated place.

The main advantages of synthetic ropes over the natural-fiber types are strength and protection from rot and mildew. Nylon 1/4-inch rope, for example, has a breaking strain of more than twice that of same-size Manila. Other synthetics rate almost as high and higher. Some synthetic ropes are unusual in that they gain rather than lose strength when wet. However, it's a rope's individual characteristics that are likely to make it highly popular for a specific job.

Dacron, for example, is used mainly aboard sailboats, where the rope's high strength, low elasticity, and good-handling properties are the advantages offsetting its high cost, which is nearly twice that of nylon. Otherwise, nylon's big competitors are polyethylene and polypropylene ropes. The polys seem to be winning out as all-purpose ropes for boats up to 20 feet. Nylon does have high elasticity, but it also has quick recovery. This spring, which apparently doesn't affect the rope's strength, is advantageous in anchor lines and dock lines, easing the shock when the boat pulls or surges suddenly.

The polys, particularly polyethylene, are very light in weight. Polyethylene weighs only 1.25 pounds for a 100-foot length of 1/4-inch line. This light weight, coupled with the rope's nonabsorbent qualities, allows it to float in the water rather than sink as other types do. This is an important plus in a line used for water skiing, towing, or anchoring. With ordinary nonfloating types, there is always the chance of a submerged line tangling the propeller. This flotation feature can also be a money saver should your anchor line accidentally get away from you.

Synthetic ropes, particularly polyethylene, are very slippery when wet. Knots and hitches tend to loosen, and splicing may require special equipment and know-how. Though polyethylene is high priced in comparison with Manila, it is still popular because it costs about a third less than nylon. Polyethylene averages 5¢ per foot for 1/4-inch diameter, up to 19¢ for 1/2-inch.

The differences among the various types of rope in strength and pricing, along with the fact that the price per foot of any line tends to double for every 1/4-inch size jump, will undoubtedly have an effect on your thinking. Rope is measured by circumference as well as by the diameter. While the diameter has become the common size designation in this country, it is still important to be specific. When ordering, for example, specify 1/2-inch diameter and the type of rope.

Nylon and polyethylene ropes, and the synthetic types generally, are twice as strong as the natural-fiber ones, including good grade Manila. The synthetics also cost twice as much or more. So, where 3/8-inch or 1/2-inch Manila would seem right for an anchor line, why not buy polyethylene or nylon in the 1/4-inch size? The strength would be equal, the cost about the same, and you'd have the good features of a synthetic rope. This line of reasoning is sound, if not carried to extremes.

In buying rope, don't go entirely by the strength-rating figures. A boat's painter and a large outboard's anchor line and dock lines should not only be strong enough but also easy to handle. The larger the line, within reason, the easier it will be on your hands, particularly when wet, and the more effectively you can haul on it.

Equally important, wear and natural deterioration should be considered. Any line will get smaller in diameter and lose some strength as it is used. Line chafe is inevitable and will tend to wear down surface fibers. Short lengths of hose, split down one side and placed over the line at any point of contact, or manufactured shields of this sort, are worth having aboard. Since

WHIPPING ENDS

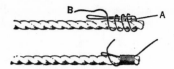

Whipping ends of lines keeps them neat. Using 2 feet of cord, wind B tight around loop, tuck B through loop, pull on A to bury the end, then clip ends.

SQUARE KNOT

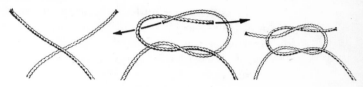

Sketch shows square knot, which is useful in joining two lines securely.

CLOVE HITCH

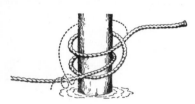

Clove hitch is used to tie a dock line to a piling. The dotted line shows an optional step with end of line to further secure the hitch.

ROLLING HITCH

The rolling hitch will not slide under a downward pull. If end is tucked under (dotted line), a yank on end will release hitch.

BOWLINE KNOT

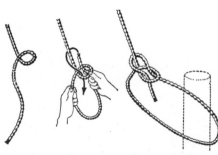

Bowline makes an eye that won't slip. Form a loop, then run end behind and through loop, around shank, and back into loop. Adjust for size, pull tight.

SECURING TO CLEAT

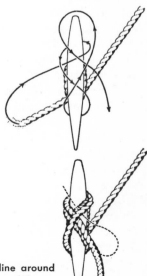

Anchor bend knot is used to secure line to anchor ring. End is lashed to line.

In tying to cleat, wrap line around base, make figure 8 around horns. Follow dotted line for quick-release.

stretch and strain eventually result in some loss in size, it's wise to take this into account when selecting rope strength.

When deciding what length of rope to buy, it's wise to buy a length that might prove too long rather than too short. In deciding anchor-line length, consider the greatest depths you're likely to anchor in. Multiply the figure by seven and add another 10 feet. That is, for the usual 10 to 12-foot soundings, you'd buy about 100 feet.

For docking, you should have at least two lines. One should be the length of your boat plus 3 or 4 feet to allow for splicing an eye in the end, or for the hitch or knot you'll otherwise use. If you'll be up against changing water levels, either a tidal range or fluctuating river stages, buy enough extra rope to allow for this. For example, a 15-footer in water with a 5-foot tidal range needs a 25-foot dock line. The second line should be half again as long. Having this two-way choice of length will often come in handy. With a larger boat which cruises extensively and uses strange docks, duplicate this set. As often as not, the berth you'll be assigned will have its catwalk or narrow dock with two tie piles off it. Then, for your boat to lie comfortably and not bang the dock, it must be held off by an extra line quartered off from the bow and another from the stern out to the piles. Or, where you must remain at a long-face dock, you'll use one of these extra lines as a spring, along with bow and stern lines, to keep the boat more exactly in position.

Once you have your lines, rig them so they can be used conveniently. Splicing a large eye in one end of each dock line will make docking easier. The eye is simply looped over a dock cleat or piling.

Manila rope is quite simple to splice. Nylon, particularly if the grade is stiff, takes more skill, one difference being that the ends of its unlaid strands must be taped or heat-fused against untwisting. Also, with any synthetic rope, its slippery nature makes five sets of tucks—rather than the usual three—essential for a strong splice.

Above all, have the plain ends of your lines neatly finished. Cowtail or bushy, unraveled ends are inexcusable. Tape the end, if you can't do better. Or, with synthetic rope, use heat from a candle's flame to fuse the cut fibers and strands solidly together. With any type of line, though, a properly applied twine whipping lasts longest and looks best (see sketch).

An easy approach to neat lines is to find someone who is a rope enthusiast. Many boat owners do this as a fascinating hobby and are often glad to put their skill to practical use.

Gradually, learn to use the proper knot or hitch for each job. The few simple ones in the accompanying sketches will suffice. The square knot is for joining two ends, the clove hitch for tying to a piling, and the bowline forms an unslipping eye or loop in the end of a line. One sketch also shows the proper way to secure a line to a cleat. These knots and hitches won't fail under strain, nor will they be difficult to untie.

22 Where to Keep It

ONE OF YOUR most important decisions is going to be where to keep your boat. To get the most out of your investment, your boat must be where you can get it under way quickly and easily. Such a set-up gives you a big advantage over owners who can't get their boats moving without first expending a lot of time and effort.

The whole question hinges on where—and how—you keep your boat between times that you're aboard.

Normally, there are these choices open to you: (1) keep it on a trailer, (2) provide your own space, or (3) rent space.

It is also important, in making your choice, that you avoid getting into a rut. Many owners do. This leads to complaining that they're not getting as much fun from their boats as they think they should. The reason is often simple—they've exhausted the possibilities offered by their approach to boating. A different approach will open new possibilities and almost invariably will renew interest.

Many boat owners, for instance, continue to use their boats on small or unattractive waters when—by simply using a trailer or hiring someone to haul their boat to another location—they could enjoy a great variety.

KEEP IT ON A TRAILER

As pointed out in the chapter on trailers, by including this piece of equipment in your total outfit, you gain maximum mobility. By investing wisely in a good trailer, you enjoy convenience over the years that more than offsets the initial cost.

If your approach to boating depends on a trailer, make it a good one. It should be of ample capacity for your boat and motor, plus whatever extra gear you'll load aboard.

If you can leave the loaded trailer in your back yard, driveway, or garage, you'll avoid storage charges. However, if you use certain launching sites, there'll likely be a charge of $1 or so.

With your boat at home, you can work on it at odd times. A proper cover, incidentally, simplifies cleaning and other maintenance.

Despite theses advantages, there are cases where a trailer won't work out so well. This may be true if you live in a crowded residential area, particularly

Trailer allows you wide choice of waters.

if you live in an apartment house. If that is your situation, investigate the possibility of storing your loaded trailer at a highway service station on the outskirts of town, or perhaps you can rent covered shed space near the waters where you most often launch.

There's a growing number of owners who use trailers in conjunction with semipermanent storage. Some have their own trailers, others depend on renting or borrowing. Many dealers have used trailers that they'll rent; you can generally find one that will fit your boat. Or some dealers—and boat-moving concerns—will take over the entire job of moving your boat from one place to another, at so much per mile. Often an owner will base his boat on some popular body of boating water during the summer, and move it elsewhere for use during the fall or spring months.

On the other hand, trailers are sometimes used when there's no real need. If there's a large and attractive body of water within reasonable driving distance, you may prefer to make that your more-or-less permanent boating area, leaving your boat there and avoiding the worry of trailering through heavy traffic. Also, as you move up to a larger-sized boat, you may feel she is getting too heavy and unwieldy to tax your car. You are now faced with the task of selecting a permanent mooring. Important considerations will be convenience—which will be reflected in how often you use the boat; and how safe it will be to leave it when you return home.

However you go about keeping your boat, the main point is to have it convenient to get into and go in attractive surroundings. Most of us, because we like to ramble ashore or camp there occasionally, consider not only the water itself but also the shoreline.

How about the fishing? If you're an avid fisherman you'll overlook some of a waterway's shortcomings if it provides good fishing.

What's your boat made of? A simple wooden one may leak unless left in the water. But that doesn't mean you can't move it from one small body of water to another. Most modern boats—notably those of fiberglass, metal, molded plywood, and the majority of panel-plywood craft—are either easier to maintain or will last longer if kept out of water between trips. Many of the better all-wood boats have been greatly improved in this respect.

With your particular interests in mind, check your immediate section for boating possibilities. Also investigate surrounding sections. Make up your mind how far you're willing to drive. Let's say 100 miles. Draw a circle of that radius on your road map.

Investigate, systematically, all bodies of water within the circle which might afford space for keeping your boat. You will then have two main avenues open to you—provide your own space by purchasing or leasing property and building your own, or rent space at commercial boating facilities.

PROVIDE YOUR OWN SPACE

If there is space available and you can arrange for access, a permanent mooring might serve your purpose. The chapter on Anchoring and Mooring explains several methods of putting down a permanent mooring. In areas where waterfront property is not priced out of reason, consider the convenience of an onshore installation.

Docks, and floats, as well as boathouses and other shelters, can be bought ready-made from many manufacturers. Many you can install yourself. If you intend to build your own from scratch, the Outboard Boating Club of America has two helpful booklets: 1. Private Boat Houses and Docks. 2. Small Boat Launching Ramps, Docks and Piers. Write to O.B.C., 333 N. Michigan Ave., Chicago 1, Ill.

Quite often, one of the main reasons for forming an outboarding club is to get better boating facilities. All members join in the cost and do their share

Private facilities may be as plush as this.

To keep your boat on good fishing water, try to make a deal with the owner of some out-of-the-way waterfront property.

of the work putting in the dock and eventually a clubhouse. Still another popular idea is to make an arrangement with some owner of a waterside place; you put in and maintain the dock or float, and he too has the right to use it.

RENTING SPACE AT A MARINA

Unfortunately, some of the larger commercial facilities do not welcome, nor have franchises and services, for small boats and outboard motors. And you may find situations where demand exceeds supply and the charges are

Typical of many small-craft marinas is this 300-boat setup, Ocean Beach, N.J.

out of reason. In those areas, investigate the possibility of keeping your boat at some out-of-the-way or small-town facility.

The demand for better storage and service facilities is rapidly multiplying, and many alert municipalities and private operators are endeavoring to meet it. The availability and quality of such services, however, vary widely. Most such places offer some sort of in-the-water storage plan for summers, plus covered winter storage.

Some supply what's called in-and-out storage, a type that perhaps suits small boats best. Your boat is assigned a space in a storage shed ashore. When you want to use the boat, an overhead trolley or fork lift is used to move out the boat. When you're through with the boat, you leave it at the dock and it's moved back into the shed.

The big advantage of this in-and-out storage is the minimum exposure to weather. And if salt-water use is involved, there's no real need to keep the boat's bottom specially painted against worms nor—if it's a metal or plastic craft—against barnacles and other bottom fouling.

If you prefer to keep your boat out of the water, salt-water storage places quite often require you to supply your own trailer for moving the craft in and out, and for storing. Trailers about such places are used more for storage in an attended parking area rather than for actual highway use.

In-the-water or "wet" storage may be either in the open or covered. The advantage of covered storage is that the boat is kept clean, and topside and inside finishes—protected against the sun and weather—stand up well. The usual way is to erect a simple shelter over the slip or dock space. Covered

"Wet" storage eliminates weekly trailering but tends to restrict area you cover.

Boats using in-the-water or "wet" storage are sheltered from dirt and weather.

or not, in-the-water storage has this advantage over storage ashore: with a larger boat, and particularly a cabin craft, there'll be times when you can enjoy your boat without leaving the dock. One main requirement for in-the-water storage is a location that's well sheltered from high winds.

Added services that you might find attractive would be fresh water and electricity available at the dock, and perhaps showers and laundry facilities on shore. Check on the availability of such supplies as ice, groceries, refreshments, and bait within easy walking distance.

The way to size up any place, of course, is to talk with other owners and visit the place before making your arrangements. Find out about the rates, and just what is, and isn't, included, preferably getting a contract form or literature to study before signing up. Find out what work you can hire done, and what arrangements you can make for working on the boat yourself. Find out about any boating restrictions.

What's the situation in your section regarding municipally owned ramps, docks, and boat basins? All over the country, waterside communities are putting in boating facilities. These range from simple launching sites to complete marinas offering all boating services.

Municipalities seldom act spontaneously in such matters. If your town is backward in its attitude toward boating, do your part to correct this situation. Possibly someone has already taken the lead. You can add your support by joining your nearest boating club, or getting together with other owners to form such a club. Let one of your aims be to work for a better boating situation.

In an early classic example, a Florida city was encouraged to install a total of three public launching ramps with enclosed areas for parking cars and empty trailers, all put in at the insistence of local boat owners and fishermen. The first resulted from a survey of civic spending for recreational purposes. The figures showed that considerable money was being spent

170

annually on maintaining city-owned golf links and tennis courts, but nothing was being done for boat owners and fishermen. Yet the golfers and tennis players were spending little on their sports in comparison to what the boatmen and fishermen were putting out for goods and services they needed.

Armed with the facts and figures, it was easy to sell the city fathers on putting in a single installation to determine the actual interest. It was so well patronized that before long two other projects were under way.

Often there's a piece of otherwise worthless city property that can be utilized with municipally owned equipment, and street or park department labor used for the filling, building, and landscaping.

Two important boating organizations are ready to offer you an effective program for your community. They're the Outboard Boating Club of America, 333 N. Michigan Ave., Chicago 1, Ill., and the National Association of Engine and Boat Manufacturers, Inc., 420 Lexington Ave., New York 17, N.Y. They can furnish information on how to organize and create local interest in municipally owned boating facilities, how to put your proposal before the proper authorities, and can supply facts on the actual engineering and construction of installations of different types and sizes of marinas.

23 Winter Storage

IF THERE'S an off-season in your area—when you have to winterize your boat and motor and put them in storage—don't wait until the last minute to make your plans. Don't, however, lay them up so early that you needlessly shorten your season and deprive yourself of the best cruising weather and some top late-season fishing.

In northern latitudes, it used to be that short-term insurance encouraged hauling out of pleasure boats and consequent abandonment of waterways before the end of October. For the sportsman with a small boat, it meant the waterways were left uncrowded at one of the most pleasant times of the year. For the trailer-boatman who could get in and out in a hurry, those delightful days of Indian Summer didn't find him high and dry. This trend has been changing in recent years. More big-boat owners are extending their season, and the insurance companies are conforming with more liberal policies.

Most sportsmen store their small boats at home during the off-season. If you can do this, you will avoid not only storage bills but also costly yard bills for work that you enjoy doing yourself. It will also give you the opportunity of tinkering over the inactive season, building custom fittings, lockers, and portable boxes for tools, tackle, bait, and grub.

For small boats, the question often becomes whether to store the boat indoors or out. Often indoor storage can be harmfully dry. On the other hand, with a well-ventilated cover, a boat left out-of-doors is apt to react best to the natural moisture supplied by Nature's weather changes.

A boat that is properly covered will allow no rain or snow to gain entrance, yet will have enough ventilation to prevent sweating. The cover should be braced on a strong frame which won't sag or collect puddles.

All hatches, doors, lazarettes, lockers, and drawers should be left open so that air can circulate freely.

Remove all loose gear. You will reduce the possibility of theft and it will give you the opportunity to inspect, clean, and repair the equipment usually overlooked until worn out—things like flashlights, radios, compass, etc. Remove anchor lines and dock lines, rinse in fresh water and hang them where they will dry and be well ventilated. Remove cushions, wash with mild soap, rinse and allow to dry thoroughly in sun and air.

Convertible tops and canvas weather cloths should be rinsed with fresh water. If they require more than mere rinsing, wash them with a canvas cleaning solution, then treat with the waterproofing and mildew inhibitor recommended by the manufacturer. If there are metal zippers on your enclosure, clean and lubricate them thoroughly. Before storing this equipment, be sure it is all bone dry and then put it where it will stay that way.

If you have a plexiglass windshield, wash it with mild soap and a soft cloth. Minor scratches can be removed with a plastic cleaner-polish or automobile paste wax. Tar, grease, or paint can be removed with naphtha or kerosene. *Do not* use acetone, gasoline, or household glass cleaners on plexiglass.

Carefully check all the hardware on your boat. Clean and polish, replacing broken fittings and tightening all loose fastenings.

If you have varnished surfaces—on seats, bulkheads, doors, drawers, or frames, go over them carefully. Light sanding and a coat of varnish will keep the finish from deteriorating. If you let those surfaces go too long, the exposed wood will darken and then you'll have a real refinishing job to do.

Clean the bottom first. If you are a trailer-boatman, you should do this after each use. If the boat has been used in fresh water only, it should be a simple matter to scrub off the accumulated slime. If it has been kept in salt water for any length of time, it will have collected barnacles and mussels. These can best be scrubbed and scraped off if you go after them immediately with fresh water. The longer you wait, the harder it will be to get rid of them.

Wash and rinse the topsides; clean the deck and cockpit sole. Then flush, drain, and clean out the bilge. Be sure to leave floorboards or hatches open to expose all areas to fresh air.

A wooden boat is considered to be as good as its surface. If it is protected by paint or varnish, it should theoretically last forever. Its chief enemy is dry

By keeping your rig shipshape, you minimize the seasonal jobs of preparing for winter storage and spring launching.

rot and this can occur anyplace where fresh water can accumulate. Carefully built wooden boats will have been treated with a penetrating preservative, otherwise all of those little cracks and crannies that you can't get to will be potential breeding grounds for destructive fungus. You can help prevent the start of dry rot by providing good ventilation throughout the hull and by periodic maintenance.

Modern aluminum alloys resist corrosion. The shallow pitting that occurs in unpainted aluminum does not weaken the metal, and it can be prevented by painting. If yours is a painted aluminum boat, consult your dealer before attempting any touch up or repainting—it is important that the materials used be compatible with one another.

If you have a fiberglass hull, after it has been washed and rinsed, clean and wax it as you would your automobile.

If yours is an inflatable boat, store it partially inflated in a cool and dry place—avoid dampness and direct sunlight. If it's a folding boat, remove the frame. One manufacturer recommends that rubber surfaces have a protective coat of liquid wax applied and when that dries, a dusting with talcum powder.

When storing a boat for any length of time, consider the fact that in its watery home it is supported completely in an element that conforms perfectly to its shape. Be sure that you also provide it with sufficient support to maintain its intended shape. Penalty for carelessness in this respect can be permanent and harmful distortion of the hull.

Normally a trailerable boat will be supported adequately over winter on the trailer that does the job properly on the highway. Heavier boats, however, do best on cradles. Often larger boats are delivered on cradles which will serve the purpose.

If you construct a cradle, the design is limited only by your own imagination. The main consideration is that it should provide form-fitting braces under centers of weight. You might design a cradle with through bolts so that it can be taken down and stored flat when not in use.

Use large pieces of cardboard to make templates for the shape of the bearing members of your cradle. Hold the cardboard perpendicular to the hull at the point to be supported and scribe the shape with a pair of dividers; cut out the section and when you have duplicated the shape, transfer it to the cradle's bed and make the cut.

Bevel the runners and chamfer their ends, possibly fitting them with metal strips so the cradle will slide easily when you want to move it.

Be sure the cradle is kept on high and solid ground that won't wash out.

When you store a boat on its trailer, jack up the trailer and boat and put the trailer axle on blocks so the weight doesn't rest on the tires. Prop up the trailer tongue so the boat rests in its normal attitude, but slightly tilted so that it will drain.

The way you treat your outboard motor during an inactive winter period can make a big difference in its performance the next spring. Don't put a motor away without proper service. If you're inclined to put off the job, get it to your dealer. He has the equipment and know-how to properly service and store your motor until spring. By leaving it with him over the winter, he can service it during his less-active period so that you're certain to be ready to go in the spring when other procrastinators line up for his help.

If you are going to do the job, follow these steps:

If the motor has been used in salt water, flush it in fresh water by operating it briefly in a freshwater tank or attach a hose to the water intake.

Remove the portable remote fuel tanks, and empty them.

Idle the motor to run fuel out of the lines and carburetor, then remove the motor from the water.

Remove drain plug, gearcase, and driveshaft housing plugs and tilt the motor from side to side to allow water to drain out.

Rinse off the motor housing; spray the head with a light film of rust preventive; give the shroud a protective coat of automobile wax; and wipe the lower unit with an oily rag.

With a spark-plug wrench, remove the plugs, pour about a tablespoon of light oil into each port. Ground the spark-plug leads and crank the engine about ten revolutions to distribute the oil over the cylinder walls.

Reseat the spark plugs and wipe the ignition wires and connections.

Clean the carburetor screens, fuel filter, and sediment bowl.

Change grease in lower unit and lubricate its linkage, the control linkage, engine swivel, and tilt mechanism.

Remove propeller and coat the shaft with a light film of grease.

Mount the motor on a stand in an upright position and in a dry place, and cover it with a plastic dust shield.

Remove the battery and clean the top with a solution of baking soda in water, then rinse with fresh water. Fill the cells with distilled water and charge to manufacturer's specifications. Store it in a cool, dry place where it will be well ventilated. Check it with a hydrometer once a month and give it a trickle charge if necessary.

If you've moved up to inboard or stern-drive power, you're now dealing with a four-cycle engine and winterizing or lay-up is quite a bit more involved and difficult, and beyond the scope of this book. Chances are you're going to rely on your dealer or a competent yard to do your hauling and lay-up. If you insist on doing it yourself, study the owner's manual and be sure to follow the manufacturer's recommendations to the letter.

24 Ready for Spring

IF YOU stored your boat properly at the end of the season, you shouldn't have much work to do on it to get it ready for service in the spring.

Any necessary work should be planned with three objectives in mind: 1. To maintain the equipment in safe, dependable condition. 2. To forestall midseason breakdowns and the need for expensive and time-consuming repairs. 3. To prolong the life of the rig and to preserve its sale or trade-in value.

The extent and nature of maintenance to be done varies greatly among boats and depends largely on the construction of the craft, its age, and the care it has been given while both in and out of service. The over-all aim should be to do what is necessary with a minimum of cost and effort. No one should become a slave to his boat.

The entire effort can best be managed by practicing preventive maintenance, which means anticipating faults that might possibly develop and doing what is necessary to prevent them from happening. In this way you can detect trouble spots and correct them in early, easy-to-fix stages.

Most maintenance problems can be solved by using proper products designed to overcome them. Marine paint and varnish will outlast ordinary paint and varnish. Copper or antifouling paint, a special marine product, is made for the purpose of safeguarding a wood hull against worms and discouraging barnacles and grass growths from adhering to the bottom.

Regardless of construction, a boat that is left in the water for long periods should have antifouling paint on its hull, and a fresh coat should be applied each spring, even more frequently if the boat is used year-round.

If the boat is kept on a trailer between trips, a special bottom paint shouldn't be necessary. If the hull is merely slimy, it can be kept clean by hosing or washing, preferably while the slime is still wet. If the condition appears more serious, however, you should use copper paint.

If painting and varnishing are necessary, it is well to remember that some types of fillers, paints, and other similar preparations, particularly those made of synthetic materials, are intended for use only on certain surfaces and with compatible solvents and primers. One product may not work well with another, and it doesn't pay to use something that's incompatible with the products originally used by the factory. If you suspect there may be something special about your boat and the products needed to maintain it, write to the manufacturer for information. Most reputable boat manufacturers put out maintenance booklets. If you don't have one for your boat, write for it. Even if special preparations are not required, as is the case with most wood boats, use good products intended for marine work. It's a good idea to read the fine print on labels and to follow instructions.

DON'T STINT ON PREPARATORY WORK

Plan to do your painting under as nearly ideal working conditions as you can. If you can do it under a shelter, fine. If not, be alert against early dew catching the surface before the paint has set. Otherwise, the sandpapery effect resulting from dew may take two coats to show smooth.

If you work on the boat in your yard, you'll most likely have access to a hose and fresh water. Otherwise, you should have at least clean creek water for washing your boat before starting a paint job. Getting it perfectly clean is a must if you want satisfactory results. Attempting to conceal dirt with paint is a waste of time and money. And you shouldn't depend on just sanding alone to prepare a surface for painting.

Don't sand a surface that could have salt on it. Sanding forces greasy dirt or salt into the old paint, making for poor adhesion of fresh paint. Instead, wash thoroughly, then sand. If the surface has been waxed, make certain the film is completely removed, using a suitable solvent. Also use a solvent on any tar or oil spots which still show after washing. Don't use an unnecessarily strong detergent, and always finish by flushing the area thoroughly with fresh water.

With the boat perfectly clean you'll be better able to check its condition. If there is any doubt that the old finish will last the season through, apply a thin coat now to prevent further deterioration. If there are bare spots, but the surface is generally in good condition, spot painting and later applying a single coat over all is better than applying two full coats.

Before you begin to paint or varnish, do a good sanding job. If the old paint is in good condition, sand lightly with fine paper. If it's only fair, use medium-grit paper and more pressure. If it is poor, use paper coarse enough to cut scaled or loose paint. It may be necessary to use a scraper on the worst areas. If so, be careful not to cut into the surface and remove any scraper marks by sanding them down.

When the surface is finally sanded and dusted clean, check for places that need filling. Fill them so that the surface is a trifle higher than the adjoining area. If there are any open seams, use a softer compound in them, but keep the filling just below the surface. The filler used on the low spots should be a quick-hardening product to permit sanding it flush with the surface after a reasonable length of time. While you're at it, sand the entire surface again very lightly, and finally retouch all bare spots with paint. Then you're ready for the final coat, which should be applied evenly and preferably under favorable weather conditions.

If the job involves using several different colors, your work will be slowed up. Each color must be neatly cut in. Cut in with the darker color, applying the lighter or white first, and using masking tape to get a sharp, even line.

Fiberglass—Using a special cleaner sold for the purpose may get rid of stains or mottling on fiberglass surfaces. A fiberglass polish will restore the luster. If the fiberglass has been painted, use good fillers and paints to touch up bare spots. If you work carefully, you can even build up badly chafed areas. If there is much of this to be done, however, or if the boat needs major repairs, work with a fiberglass-repair kit. If you have an unpainted fiberglass boat and it looks O.K. after a good cleaning and polishing, don't paint it.

Should you decide to paint, however, remember that it's essential to give the paint every chance to adhere to fiberglass. Sand the surface to give it "tooth"—a uniform dullness, even a rough feel. After dusting it, wipe it clean with the solvent of the finish you'll be using. Follow the boat manufacturer's instructions on the temperature at which to work, primers or undercoats, and number of coats necessary for thorough coverage. If paint already on the boat shows signs of peeling, the only real remedy is to strip it off completely, using paint or varnish remover, and then repaint.

Aluminum—With bare aluminum, that grayish dull appearance is normal. It's surface oxidation and not an indication of deterioration. After a thorough washing, leave the surface dull or try polishing it. If you decide to paint the boat, get complete directions from the manufacturer. The surface must be specially cleaned, prepared, and primed or paint will not retain its hold.

If the boat is already painted but has spots where bare metal shows, each spot should be primed with an aluminum primer and then touched up to match the surrounding surface. If the old paint is in bad condition, don't attempt to doctor it up. It is not hard to strip an aluminum hull if you use a modern, marine-type remover. You can then do a good job of tapping out dents and make other repairs. The boat's manufacturer is your best source of supply for materials and directions when major repairs are required.

Canvas—If a canvas craft is less than five years old and was built by a reputable firm, there is a good chance that its covering was specially treated and finished. In some cases, the finish is meant to be rejuvenated after so many years, using a set technique and special products available from the boat's manufacturer. It's sensible to ask the company about methods and materials.

Aside from this, the secret of maintaining a canvas-covered surface is not to paint too much. If a thorough washing will do, fine. If you must paint, clean and sand the old paint thoroughly. By touching up bad spots first, try to make a single, over-all coat do. If painted canvas shows cracks, alligatoring, or flaking, you're wasting your time and money if you try to doctor up the paint job. If the canvas is still good, strip off the old paint with remover, but be careful not to cut the canvas when scraping. Then build up a new coating with several coats of paint. Sand lightly between coats. If the canvas itself shows dark, pencillike lines in square patterns, a condition known as checking, you can be sure moisture has got into the fabric and that it has begun to rot. New paint applied over such a surface will show checks in the same places a year or so later. Where checking is apparent, it is wise to remove the old fabric completely and put on a new covering.

Wood—The maintenance of wood boats, including plywood, seldom calls for special products or techniques, but it is a good idea to spend considerable time on preparation—thorough washing, sanding, filling or puttying—before painting. Except possibly where bottom paint is to be applied, the wood itself must be thoroughly dry, not just the surface. Don't spend time and money trying to do a decent job if the old paint is too far gone. Remove it and start fresh.

This applies particularly to varnished surfaces. If the varnish is discolored or coming off the wood in spots, complete removal, careful sanding, and a fresh varnishing are indicated. Varnished surfaces cannot be patched. Even if old varnish is in good condition, apply three or four fresh coats at the beginning of the season. A single coat may restore brightness, but the surface will show serious faults by midseason. Varnishing differs from painting in that the more coats you apply the better.

Plywood rarely delaminates now that waterproof plywood is the rule in boat construction. Delamination causes bulges in the outside plys and cracks between plys along edges. Checking—minute surface cracks—is still a rather common fault. Paint often checks when the wood underneath is affected. Sanding and repainting, even when the many small checks are carefully filled, gives only temporary relief. Remove the old paint, sand and fill, seal the surface with several coats of special plywood sealer, and then apply several coats of paint.

Faults that go beyond routine painting are an entirely different matter. Rot seldom shows up until a boat gains age, but leaks or structural weaknesses may appear in a relatively new boat. A hull may start to alter its shape, perhaps developing a hook in the bottom astern. Anything of this nature should be fixed as soon as it is detected. If you don't know how to do it yourself, search out a reputable boat carpenter and have him give you an estimate on what it would cost to make good the fault.

When structural faults develop, it is sometimes wiser to consider trading in the boat rather than having a repair job done since the cost of skilled boat labor can run surprisingly high. A dealer can often give you a trade-in allowance that will leave you better off in the long run.

MECHANICAL MAINTENANCE

The battery should be inspected and brought to full charge. If the condition of the battery is doubtful, it's best to replace it. In any case, terminals must be free of corrosion to insure proper contact. If you install the battery yourself, be sure you connect the proper cables to the proper terminals. Use a battery box with tie-down strap.

Examine all electrical connections and switches. Check all wiring for cracked, chafed, or broken insulation. Turn the key switch on and off and if it's not right, replace it. Remove bulbs in lights and clean the contacts. Replace burned-out bulbs and cracked lenses, and, if needed, put in new rubber or cork gaskets.

If there is a control box, disassemble it, clean it out, and relubricate. Replace broken nylon racks and kinked cables. Work the cables until free before hooking up to the motor.

Go over the steering system. If it has cables and pulleys, examine the cables for fraying, damage, and bad alignment. The cables should lie flat on the drum of the steering wheel and pull through the pulleys easily. All pulleys should be at least 2-inches in diameter for easy steering and so that they will not damage the cable. Proper tension is necessary to assure positive control and elimination of wear. Oil the pulleys and wheel.

Get rid of any fuel left over from last year. Be sure the fuel tank is clean inside and out. Gum and varnish deposited inside the tank can be removed with lacquer thinner. Put a dozen half-inch pebbles in the tank along with a quart of thinner and agitate briskly. The pebbles will break up the deposits so the thinner can go to work. Flush thoroughly with clear gas.

Check the fuel-line connections for proper fit at the tank and at the motor. Make sure there are no kinks or abrasions and that the line is not cramped or restricted in any way.

If your boat is a sizable one, it will have a fair amount of equipment that should be checked. Tighten or replace any loose fastenings holding hardware or parts. Check accessories with moving parts, notably the steering and motor controls, looking for poor fastening, chafe, and faulty lubrication. Here you should follow the manufacturer's instructions concerning installation and maintenance.

If your motor was properly stored last fall, it should easily start and run upon refueling. Even so, for easy starting and all-season dependability, it should get an over-all check.

Start with the fuel system. If the tank, lines, and carburetor were drained and flushed, a check to see that all connections are tight should suffice. If you neglected doing a thorough cleaning job last fall, follow the manufacturer's instructions for using a solvent. A fuel system should be flushed until all traces of foreign matter are removed. Then, if possible, blow compressed air through the system. And don't refuel with any gas left over from last year; start out with new.

Next, check the electrical system. Remove any oil you may have placed in the cylinders last fall. When taking out the spark plugs, be sure to hold the wires against some part of the motor, to ground the magneto, before engaging the starter. If you don't ground the wires you may damage the magneto. If the condition of the plugs warrants it, have them cleaned and the gaps reset. But if the porcelain is cracked or the electrodes are burned down, install new plugs. While you're at it, look for deterioration of the spark plug leads, particularly where the insulation comes in contact with metal parts. If rubber insulators are cracked, replace them. Finally, check plug connections for possible corrosion. If the magneto requires attention, the job is best left to your dealer or outboard service station who'll have special equipment for the work. The same applies to your motor if it has a generator or alternator. Follow the manufacturer's instructions as to lubricating and possibly tightening the belt, but avoid overdoing either.

Go over all nuts, screws, and connections, tightening and replacing where needed. Be sure that the fly-wheel nut is tight, using a proper wrench, not pliers. Have an oil can handy and, using No. 30 motor oil, apply a few drops to control linkage points, levers, bushings, and all moving parts beneath the cowl.

Check the lubricant in the lower unit and, if necessary, refill using the recommended grade. Remove the propeller, and check for nicks and rough places along the blade edges. If there are any, file them smooth. If there's any chance of the wheel being out of balance from having hit something, have your dealer check it. Smear a little waterproof grease on the shaft before replacing propeller. If the motor uses a shear pin, replace it if it is bent or nicked. When you're finished, wipe the motor clean and touch up any spots where the paint has been chipped or is worn off.

Finally, check all accessories. On remote fuel tanks, inspect the hose and make sure all fittings are tight. If the gasket on the filler cap looks worn, replace it. When you connect the motor, recheck the steering and control systems to see that everything works smoothly. If there's a battery, have it looked over and brought up to charge.

Last, but not least, don't neglect your trailer. Refer to the chapter on trailers.

By inspecting regularly and correcting minor faults as they develop, your outfit will always be dependable and ready to run. Once a rig is in good shape, it is easy to keep it so season after season.

INDEX